The Desperate Days of Doyle

An Introverts Guide to Ecommerce

Doyle C. Carver

DEDICATION

To Sandi Rochelle Carver

Hey baby, we made it this far! Who would have thought it, eh? Your hard work certainly sealed the deal. Thank you more than I know how to say. Cheers to you and to the next mountain, wherever it may be.

Dictionary via Google

"Desperate"

…Despairing, Desperation, Desperado, last ditch, last gasp, do or die, frantic, frenzied, wild, a near futile effort in the face of hopelessness, when everything else has failed and having little hope of success………

"Introvert"

……..a person who is energized by spending time alone. Not always shy, but intensely needing time alone. Need for private recharge…………..

Urban Dictionary.

Contents

Dedication 3

Acknowledgments 6

1 Being Out Of Work Changes Everything 7

2 Starting From Little To Nothing 13

3 Paying For My Education 21

4 Ecommerce For Introverts 38

5 Working It..48

6 Continuing Education (Or All The Other Stuff They Didn't Tell You About)..61

7 Some Things Don't Sell Or The List Of Shame........ 71

8 Avoiding Competition Or Sailing For The Blue Ocean 80

9 At A Show Or Wielding The Cash Strapped Check Book...84

10 Bringing The Treasure Home 91

11 Buying Deep 99

12 Building A Brand (It's Funny How Things Work Out) 103

13 The Social Side Of Things..113

14 My Future 116

ACKNOWLEDGMENTS

I'm so thankful to so many people who have helped me survive this business journey. Tom got me going, Steve straightened me out. Then a giant cast of players from the Internet Merchants Association kept me from feeling lost for the last 20 plus years. If it weren't for you guys I doubt I would be where I am today. For real.

Also special thanks to Kat Simpson for editing

And Sandi Carver for demanding to know exactly what I was talking about in each paragraph.

1 BEING OUT OF WORK CHANGES EVERYTHING

It's funny how life weaves and turns and sometimes spins out of control. How many of us can look at where we are today and say, "Yep, I planned every step I made to get to this point," then puff out our chest and follow with, "This is exactly where I expected to be!"

Yeah, not very many of us. Thankfully, my business has survived by Happy Accidents many times in my life. I only knew to go in that direction (pointing randomly) which was the only positive one I could see away from the bad spot I was in, and positive things eventually happened.

When I began to write this book I was stopped by the decision of making this a memoir or making this a business book about how I came to be here. While I certainly have a lot of memories of those days I will try and stay within the bounds of my intent to detail how my business developed from the earliest most important events. Where I'm from and what caused me to choose this way of life is important only in that it separates my story from yours. I really don't think it's necessary to describe my inability to tell time till I was eleven, or the minute detail of my kindergarten or how I stuttered terribly but could sing perfectly........and on up the years.

However, if you are just dying to know, my early family activity is being detailed in another book that is currently in progress.

Describing my history from my young adulthood and on is only interesting in that I hope it's cool to see how we all travel different paths, some not smooth at all, yet somehow wind up near the same place. This story starts from the loss of just about everything to 7 figure sales in 41 short (and sometimes desperate) years.

My family is from Arkansas and we slowly migrated to Texas during the oil booms of the 50's and 60's. I used to laughingly describe us as itinerant oil field workers. Wherever the drilling rigs moved my Dad followed in his old Chevy with trailer house pulled behind. He, my Momma, and my two brothers and I lived all over Texas in it. All this travel made us kids go to several different schools each year. I think deep down my Dad had a little gypsy blood in him so he gave little thought to uprooting whenever the opportunity came. The effect on us boys though was to always be the new kids. We got to start all over in our social circles many times. I understand military brats experienced the same type of social displacement. Maybe that's where my tendency to be an introvert came from.

The oilfield provided a living for just about all my family, from my Papaw, my Dad, and also for me when I came of age. Bad thing about the industry though is that it is cyclic and so there is always, and I mean always, a bust after a boom. The bust of the 80's caused me to lose just about everything I owned and eventually made me an oilfield refugee. I let a car and two pieces of real estate just go back to the bank. Total economic losses. I simply couldn't make the notes. The industry continued to flat line making it impossible to find any kind of work. So, I looked for other things to do for a living; anything except oilfield. I was burned out on that and even worse I didn't trust it any longer. This is when I formed my opinion that hard times are always coming in some form - I just didn't know when, and to prepare accordingly. My feeling then is mirrored in a popular saying now. "Winter is coming." The moment I heard that phrase I knew exactly what it meant. To add to these hard days I also divorced and added those continuing expenses to an already overloaded economic burden. I was becoming desperate.

While being unemployed certainly affected my bank account, it also began to affect everything else. It began to affect my health of mind. My self-image began to slip. My confidence fell away like a facade on a building. I began to think that I was never really skilled, or educated or trained in anything, despite my background in sales and extensive training in rejection (door to door sales) I couldn't find a job. I wasn't being picky either. Sad thing was, I had good company in those days, as neither machinists, carpenters, welders, nor electricians, were finding work either.

It's an incredibly depressing spot to be in. What little money I had come from selling my stuff to anyone who would buy it. I had zero negotiation ability then as no one really needed any of it. I wonder now if they didn't buy it out of charity. As I was to learn many times in my life, for want of a better explanation, God works in mysterious ways.

While I still made an effort to go to interviews when I found them, I found myself with lots of extra time on my hands while waiting. I began to stop into a small auto parts store in the mornings as I went out looking for work. They had free coffee (thank God as I was all into anything that was free) and all the free conversation I could stand. Finally after stopping there every day for months, out of sheer desperation, I wound up working at Gary's Auto Parts. For free. I'm not kidding. I just needed a place to be able to go to have something constructive to do. I started helping out there to pay for all the free coffee I drank every morning. At that time my poor friend Gary was having trouble keeping his own business open. He couldn't even pay me but still he needed a little help. Working seven days a week wears the brain and the heart out after a while. The oil bust affected everybody.

My main job at Gary's was making coffee, cleaning the counter, sweeping, and eventually answering the phone and looking up auto parts. One day in a desperate attempt to make a little more money, Gary told a customer that I could rebuild his carburetor for him. He sold the kits and filters and figured that he and I together could do it. I had only taken apart a motorcycle carburetor previously. But on the other hand this customer was willing to pay me to do it.

What the heck? Daring born of desperation.

Yes, I did need the money badly enough to try this. What's the worst that can happen? I can give the buyer his money back if it didn't work. I mean, **I was already a failure, so I had that behind me.**

One thing I know I can do is read, so I broke open the carb kit box and started reading the instructions. It didn't look too hard at all and I think the labor charge was $30. I accepted, and from that moment I was the "carb guy" of Windfern Road. I actually developed a little reputation for specializing in it. I went on to build a LOT of carbs and even took a course in the newer electronic ones and finally in throttle bodies. If you don't know what this stuff is, no matter, it's all antique by now.

I slowly learned to not only rebuild the carbs but to remove and install them and adjust them till the owner liked the way it ran enough to pay me. Still, it was only a part time income, barely a hobby. Little did I know that this was to lead me into my own shop later on.

As the oil business continued to atrophy, I started thinking that I had to do something more. Somehow, during the divorce I managed to keep my old trailer house. My ex didn't want anything to do with it. It was old and decrepit. I couldn't blame her for wanting to be rid of it. I bought her out of it in spite of not having a regular income and still managed to avoid bankruptcy. It may have been the only thing to keep me from becoming homeless.

During this time as I was having trouble paying my bills I got behind in a couple of important areas. One of them was to the IRS. Who knew that they would actually come out to my house to ask why I wasn't paying them? I remember my front lawn being hip high in grass and kid's toys scattered all over my house.   As the agent identified himself, I blurted out that I didn't have any money and he could just arrest me now. I stuck my hands out waiting for the cuffs. I was dead serious. He actually laughed a little at that. He then asked what happened. I told him that the oilfield went bad on me and several people went out of business and left me holding the bag.   I showed him a stack of unpaid invoices. I told him about how I had lost almost everything I owned and even divorced.   I told him I didn't have anything left to give him and that I was worried about how I was even going to pay child support.

Here is the miracle part.   He laid some forms out on my carpet, produced a red marker with which he drew a diagonal line across each one and then asked me to sign on the bottom of each. He then stood up with the signed forms and said, "You got bad debts, we got bad debts. Sorry for your troubles, we won't be bothering you anymore."

Though I have had several people listen to this with skepticism I want to state that angels do show up occasionally because this story is absolutely true, even if the angel was an IRS agent. Again, the only explanation I have is God works in mysterious ways.

2 STARTING FROM LITTLE TO NOTHING

I brain stormed with my buddies Gary and Gwen, owners of the auto parts store, and we decided that with my existing meager skill set, I should open a tire repair shop. There were none in the vicinity. Thankfully I had no immigrant competition in those days. You know, and I say this with a wry grin, because they say Americans won't do that kind of work. If it wasn't for the chance to open a flat repair shop with little or no competition around I'm not sure I wouldn't have been destitute after a while. So with another friend's kind financial assistance I started a small used tire shop. I bought an air compressor, an air impact wrench, tire machine, 50 used tires and painted a sign on an inner tube and placed it on the street. My self-image was about complete. All labor, all the time.

Plus this began to give me a little more experience in vehicle repair. Car repairs had always been the bane of my existence. I had spent so much money in my life on vehicles!   So, since I was selling used tires and fixing flats I just naturally started doing small things to customer's cars like changing out headlights or replacing wiper blades. Luckily I opened the shop right next door to Gary's Auto Supply.   Later, I even learned to replace brakes, water pumps, and belts and hoses.   Please understand that business was very slow but I lived in a poor neighborhood so it was slow and steady.   I honestly wasn't sure that the used tire market could support me but **when you get poor enough poor things become important.** Selling used tires and fixing flats was my way out of being totally broke and feeling useless.

It was a desperate move but **sometimes just the fact that you are moving instead of standing there helpless heals you.**

It did me, anyway.

While waiting on business to show up at my little tire shop I had another great idea.   Why not paper the neighborhoods with advertising leaflets (that's what all the other businesses did) and offer some really economic incentives to attract new customers?   I set up wiper blades, oil changes, tire balances, free tire pressure check, fluids, etc. This ought to get my name out in front of a lot of new eyes. As the day arrived for the promotion I started getting the most unfriendly and downright weird people coming in. They wanted whatever I advertised, but didn't want to spend even a penny more for anything else.   Plus they didn't want me to even look at anything else.   I was learning another great business lesson.   **When you actively set up your advertising to appeal to cheap skates, the lowest of the small-time spenders, then why be surprised when that**

is all that shows up? This one advertising failure probably saved me a small fortune from then on.

There are other ways to attract customers and one of the best was by word of mouth. Having customers recommend my service is terrifically valuable and free, but I don't mean exclusively by the referrals of my customers, but by my own mouth. **I got more work from being out and about and giving out business cards than I did with any other method.** This is back when Yellow pages advertising was popular too. It was crazy expensive in those days with high power salesmen working on you. Sure enough, I fell for it. Another business tuition payment. If Yellow Pages ever generated a single sale for me I certainly wasn't aware of it. But since it was the expected way that everybody advertised it took me several years to finally stop using it.

The take-away here? Just because it was the accepted WAY to do business did not make it the right way for me. It certainly doesn't mean I'm any less of a business man for not using it. The beginnings of my business maturity meant that I had to say NO to the common consensus and invent my own path. The common consensus is not always the right way to go.

That "job" at the parts store and then next at the tire shop probably saved me from some really dangerous tendencies I began to develop. Interject LOTS of drinking and LOTS of motorcycle riding — and gave my feet a place to stand. It's amazing to me now looking back from the distance of many years how I had the money to go out drinking at all. Somehow I came up with it.

Being a regular around the parts store and around that little corner of Windfern and Zaka Roads kept me from floating away and even now I thank God it was there. Only being 31 years old meant I had a ton of energy and so was ready to party or work at the drop of a hat.

My Dad gave me advice when I was young and starting my work life. I had been complaining about not being able to find work that paid decently. Everything was so low in those days it seemed to me. He said, **"Son, it don't matter. Just take a job, any job, because working isn't spending money.** If you don't work, the only thing you can do is spend. You will be perfectly broke in no time, but even making a little bit of money has a double advantage. One, it keeps you out of the pool halls, and two, it gives you time to look for a better job. While everyone else waits, you are gaining more experience and still have a little pocket change, even if it isn't very much."

During this time I was also a musician. I mean, with little to no work, I filled up the hours as best I could. Actually, I became a singer songwriter since I fancied myself such a writer, and spent an inordinate amount of time working at it. The problem was, it paid nearly nothing, and I being practically unemployed and broke with child support and kids to help my ex raise, the time I spent on music was just not a good trade off. Still, I worked hard at it for a long while. I used to remark in those days that I ate, slept, and dreamt music. I made a couple of self-published albums, had recordings published on some compilation albums, had a couple songs recorded by other artists, and even managed to get two songs in the Smithsonian Institute's Fast Folk archive section as an example of Americana music. We had never even heard the term before and considered ourselves

Texas music or picker poets or just plain folk singers. I think there is another category called Texana now. No matter, it was fun and enjoyable while it lasted but it didn't supply enough income for me and my family. I had to spend the time doing something else.

Adding to this part of the story I just wanted to point out that the successes I needed to see in music did not come about no matter how hard I worked. What I'm talking about is local acceptance and area acceptance. Those with the power simply weren't buying what I had to sell. For me, being near desperate for money while working at the creative side of music had a tendency to skew the writing too. I felt that my songs needed to be written without the thought of dollar signs hanging on every note. I slowly became disappointed with myself because I was spending such an immense amount of time and energy with so little to show for it. My lyrics and melodies began to be mechanical and forced. I had lost the feel to things. I did manage to come away with some great stories, friends, and a stack of 'almosts'. Like that time I was invited to Lyle Lovett's signing party, or when Peter Yarrow and I traded songs in the back of a pick-up truck during a storm or that time I sang for Townes Van Zandt's memorial in Houston. All wonderful memories and deserving mention somewhere. If you don't know who these people are, try Wiki, or Google search.

ANYWAY, I quietly showed myself the door.

You may be wondering, Hey I thought this guy was an introvert! From a very early age I fought the tendency toward introversion. When it came time to sing a song for my family, I was terrified. When it was time to read for a group.   Terrified. Whenever I had to perform in any manner in public, I was terrified and more than that I would actually lockup. I realized even as a youngster that I had to control this feeling and managed to train myself to show a calm front whenever I was in public, no matter the raging butterflies in my stomach and my heart trying to beat out of my chest. I wonder if I didn't actually enjoy that feeling as I went on to act and sing in public. Still, I worried all the way up to the moment of the performance and then breathed a huge sigh of relief when it was over. I told my wife once that my favorite part of performing was always the moment after it was over. It took me near all my life but I figured it out. Performing was simply a way to get my stuff out there. It was necessary, even if painful.

As one large life event began to wane another approached on the horizon. I got extra lucky this time. I found my partner. I say, 'found' because I certainly wasn't looking for a woman to fit in my life. I mean, I didn't have any extra money to speak of, I had two kids and my ex to support, and vehicles to maintain while she went back to school. I was busy and didn't really need the distraction of trying to keep someone else happy. I was soon to realize my mistake. **Your life partner shouldn't be that much work.** If they are, then maybe they aren't right. Right? I was about to learn another life lesson.

I have long been of the belief that our path through this world can be simply illustrated. Imagine this. The world is a long, gigantic hill and it takes our entire life to climb up it and cross it. It goes up so far you can't see the top. That is how the future works. We have to get up there, cross over, and coast down the other side. As time goes on, we begin to carry more and more things with us as we make that trip.   Possessions, children, a house, bills, everything we need to have in this world has to be carried with us.   If we are fortunate, we have a wagon which will hold lots of stuff, and if we are extremely fortunate we have a helper to pull the wagon alongside us.   Note that this partner has to be strong because every so often one may fall sick or get deathly tired and need to ride awhile.   The partner takes over and pulls till the other is ready to help again.   Pulling a wagon is so much easier with two than one. And it will make the coasting on the other side more enjoyable too.

Sandi fit in my mountain of tasks like she was made for them.   Plus she was tough, not minding hard physical work and fell in love with my kids almost immediately.   She enjoyed all my music buddies and loved going to the dives we played and coming home at bar time every other night, then up the next morning and off to work.   Seriously, it's not just anybody that could do that week after week.   As for knowing if this girl was the right one, well, it began to feel like part of me was missing when she wasn't around.   My parents loved her and so did my children.   When all my closest friends agreed with me, well, the next step was surely the right thing to do.

She agreed to marry me at the Red Lion restaurant/bar just south of downtown Houston.   It was a big party and my buddies surprised us with a gift trip to Cancun!   Damn good buddies, if I say so myself.   I still love each and every one of them to this day.

By this time my little used tire shop had morphed into a full-fledged auto repair shop.   It was just one bay in a building I rented but it supported me and my family.   So while hurrying to finish a brake job I dropped a front wheel rotor on my ankle.   It made my trip to Mexico even more memorable as I had to hobble around everywhere.   I definitely didn't climb those pyramids I had heard about. Maybe next trip if the cartels will ever stop trying to kill each other down there.

3 PAYING FOR MY EDUCATION

When I got back to the real working world we settled down to taking care of our responsibilities. My shop got busier and I hired some help. Then through the grapevine I found out that my landlord was thinking of asking me to move out. Mechanic shops are loud and dirty generally, and he was tired of that. So, my internal alarms began to go off and I started looking for a place to move my shop. Those feelings of desperation showed up in my stomach again... I felt an urgency to get out of there on my terms, not my landlord's. Surprisingly, the 1 acre lot right next door was for sale for the ridiculously outrageous price of $20,000!

I wouldn't pay it! Actually, I couldn't pay it.

I looked everywhere and could find nothing else that would work. I came back to the seller with my tail between my legs and offered him $18,000. He refused and insisted on $20k.   I gave him some down money and we were off to sign a note and then plan on pouring a slab and putting a building up.

I found out my landlord was furious that I bought that property.   He had been in negotiations with the seller for months.   Oh well, he shouldn't have threatened me with eviction.   It set my Desperation Alarm off.

This particular lesson impressed on me that when I find the right direction to go, -

Don't WAIT!

Go for it with all you got.   The more time goes by the more issues come up.   **Don't let some weird issue that's important to someone else damage what's best for your future.**   To this day I feel that speed is important, otherwise life has a way of throwing a wrench in the plans. If I determine the right way to go, I won't wait.   I suggest strongly you might consider adding this to your arsenal of business strategies.

All this was my early business education in buying land, dealing with bankers, selecting steel buildings, concrete, driveways, sewers, fence, negotiations, and hiring.   I had plenty of tuition to pay because I knew none of this stuff. As the erectors finished installing the building itself, I discovered I hadn't factored in the cost of electricity or plumbing!   I went back to the bank to borrow more money to finish the job.

They refused to loan me any more money.   They suggested I come up with more collateral. This was another lesson in the making.

I had been overly honest about my money making abilities and it cost me my banker's confidence.

Even though he had the lien on the building and property he wouldn't even give me extra money for the electrical install? Seriously? I'm not saying avoid honesty, but I am saying don't spill your guts to a banker. He/she is not your friend. He told me I could collateralize my cars for extra money. Thankfully, they were paid off. I did use them later only for that purpose. A couple of them didn't even run anymore. I just pushed them up against the back fence. They became dirty, rusty collateral that I used to borrow money for years and years. They also became prime places for my "guard" dogs to nap under during hot days. So there was that.

Back to my building problem. I didn't know exactly what to do. I priced the electrical install and got $5k to $10k in quotes. I just didn't have the money.

Finally, in desperation (there's that word again!) I walked next door to my buddy's building and studied his breaker box. I then bought a Time Life book on how to do electrical work in a house. From there I paid cash for everything and installed the entire electrical breaker box, weather head, and all wiring myself. Note that we were in county here in Texas (not in the city limits) and weren't required to hire certified installers. I did have to pass inspection and did so with flying colors. Just by looking in my next door neighbor's breaker box and reading Time Life books I managed to pull this chore off. I did have major help from my employees at that time. Vince, Stoney, Lester, and Paul were invaluable.

A note on desperation.

I have found myself desperate so many times in my life. Due to questionable life choices and sometimes due to normal chaos that comes along I would find myself with no choices. I repeated this to a friend way back and he disagreed saying I always had a choice. I said no, I didn't. He said, you could have given up on the building issue and declared bankruptcy. You could have borrowed extra money from your parents, your friends, or maybe a different bank. I told him none of those were choices I would ever make. I had already tapped all legitimate sources. As for borrowing money from my family, we have always kept finances separate. It was considered shameful if you had to even ask. Bankruptcy was not a choice for me. I realize it is a tool, but one I have tried my hardest to avoid all my life. In spite of the common consensus that it only has financial bearing for a few years I actually overheard bankers discussing it. To them it was a consideration, no matter how long ago it happened. Bankruptcy has serious negative repercussions that follow for years and years, maybe forever.

I used the only tool I had left and that was Desperation.

Desperation motivated me to go places I never thought I could or would go. What I mean by this is that I had to keep my mechanics wages paid or they would suffer. I had to keep my child support paid or my children would suffer. It was the same with keeping my ex in cars. I had motivations that could not be ignored in my mind. All these responsibilities made me look at my world with new eyes. Due to the effect of desperation I looked outside my confining box of trouble to solutions I wouldn't even have considered otherwise.

My employees help continued through my plumbing education. It was only then I began to think of installing a fence. How many things could I forget or ignore? Obviously, a lot. My guys assured me that they could build a fence and proved it by totally installing it themselves. An acre of property chain-link fenced by us and paid cash by me as I came up with it from jobs we were working on. During all this, we never closed the shop. We just couldn't. I had to have the cash to keep going. My guys had to have income too. Looking back it was amazing we did it.

Back to the plumbing. I bought another Time Life book and figured it out from there. Luckily, when the concrete form was installed the guys also installed the plumbing in it. I had given them my hen scratch sheet of planning paper. They just followed the dots. It was relatively easy to connect everything inside the building once the walls were up. We installed the hot water heater up on top of the office and to this day I don't know why we did that. The book said to do it and so did a couple of friends. What a weird place to place a hot water heater. Never again will I put something above my head that is just waiting to surprise me with a flood in my ceiling.

I just now searched EBay for Time Life Repair books and even now the first two items to come up were plumbing and electricity, available for $3.79 and free shipping. Sounds impossible but it's true. Enough education for seriously cheap to get going on any project. I know you can also find great videos on YouTube now but having a reference book on location, in hand, is very handy.

We had a building up and closed in and everything installed and built. However, I had also failed to consider the cost of an office inside and so had to build that cash also. All hard learned lessons that are filed away when/if I need them later on.

One of my biggest lessons was to plan better.

Sheesh! My sense of planning was out the window. I had expected certain things from workers, bankers, and loans without verifying hardly any of it. Another example of how that "do unto others" thing just doesn't always work.

An important thing happened in that most if not all the people I depended on didn't show up. Here's the thing; no matter what they promise, most people don't do what they say they will do. This is what began to separate me from friends and business associates. I hate it to this day, those who don't show up when they say they are going to. **I'm not sure what is wrong with them but they make themselves so easy to be dispensed with that I just naturally do.**

Sandi and I have remarked that this one particular thing follows me throughout my business life and probably my personal life too. People I rely on don't follow through. Someone says they will call me. They don't. They say they will be at my shop on a certain date. Nope. They say the papers will be ready to sign on Thursday. What papers? It seems to be evident in every facet of my life.

As I reflect on this, let me say that my realization that people won't follow through is not total. I do have an a/c guy who will be right here day or night. Also, I have a graphic artist that is on the money. I may have others I depend on to show up but I can't think of them now. That's how few there really are.

I still lacked a decent driveway from the street to the building. I had dirt brought in and made a deal with a customer who did concrete. We swapped labor on a motor install while he fixed my driveway.

Several things I took away from all this.

ONE. I can do most anything if I can study it and take the time to figure it out. Previous knowledge would have been helpful, for sure, but it certainly wasn't necessary.

TWO. While money is definitely needed to do all this, I could pay for it little by little with cash as I earned it, thereby keeping my debt low to nothing. Debt can be the great strangler of small business. Financial baby steps work amazingly well. I will talk about that in more depth in a later chapter.

THREE. My banker did not have all the power. I learned that I could stop crawling in there to beg for a loan nearly as often.

Now just to make a point here. I didn't know all the rules then and I don't know all of them now. I'm still learning. I'm still being taught. Why? Because I'm just not that smart. As long as my tuition is still being paid, hopefully, the most painful lessons are behind me. We shall see.

Another thing about being smart. It seems if you are smart enough you can pre-figure all the obstructions stopping you from great achievements. If you aren't that smart all you do is focus on the achievement. What obstructions? So, I'm admitting to being just dumb enough to succeed here. If I had been smart enough to forecast all the problems, I might not have attempted any of this. **Sometimes, thought is the enemy of action.**

From Blogger, Fish and Hickey Bar. "The Monster of Risk"

As the owner of DC Mach, I tend to run into a lot of people who want their own business. They want the perceived goods. The money. To be the boss. To have the final say, the big stick. They want freedom.

But, I guess you've heard - freedom isn't free. To the new business owner I offer some advice concerning risk.

Business is a constant reminder that everything costs either money or labor and it's not the obvious things that will kill you. It's the unknown monster that eats up both.

I'm assuming we all know what costs are involved in our businesses. Buy a widget wholesale then mark it up to retail. That cost is pretty easy to figure. Then you have rent, utilities, wages, taxes, advertising, etc. All relatively simple costs to tabulate. These are easily known.

But wait, now you have to factor some sort of cost figure for risk. This is hard to do. You have to guess what could happen to trip you up. A fire? Storm? Market collapse? Loss of key employee or distributorship? We all have varying levels of risk tolerance. I have never been able to tolerate huge risks. So I take lots of small ones. I would rather fight small monsters with a rock and a stick than giant monsters with a cannon.

It seems to me that my business has been a series of baby steps because of those unknown monstrosities. I admit, I don't know if this is the best way to go or not. Those baby steps may be why I'm not the next Bill Gates. I don't know if he took baby steps but I like to imagine he did. In my case it was a way to handle risk. I mean, why stick your head out during a hail storm when you can stick out a finger? In a worse case, like a really big bowling ball size chunk of falling hail, which part of yourself would you rather lose? At least I would be alive to try another day. I mean, I would have 9 fingers left. I honestly expect wisdom to cost me something so winding up with only 9 fingers is acceptable.

But what about those circumstances you can't plan for? The ones that stick their heads up like a tyrannosaurus rex over the trees tops. He sees you. You can fight, hide, or run. All three decisions could be the right one.

If you don't remember any more than this, please remember you will always be at risk and something will always be threatening you. When you own your own business the T Rex shows up when you least expect it. You simply can't begin to foresee all the monsters that will threaten you.

I was once sued by a county law firm for not paying property taxes on the property NEXT door. It wasn't my property and never had been. However, they didn't care and only wanted payment. They filed a lien on the property I was currently on. My taxes were paid up. I had to secure a lawyer as they really wouldn't talk to me and the court date was approaching. We settled it through him and they disappeared leaving me feeling fully justified in thinking monsters really are out to get me!

Another time we lost our water. It simply went off. We called the water company and got an answering machine. Seven days later, innumerable phone calls, walking every inch of our property and the adjacent property, we found an old house that a man was repairing. He had found a valve up under his house and had simply turned it off, not knowing it was the main line to our building. The water company didn't know this either. Being devoid of water for a week meant bathroom usage was questionable. We had to haul water in 5 gal buckets from the ditch out at the street to flush the commodes in the building. But wait, there's more.

One morning I came onto the property and only one of my working dogs came to the gate. I keep dogs mainly to just bark a lot. I believe they have been the primary reason I haven't been broken into over the years. The only insurance I've ever had that greeted me at the gate and I truly loved.

I looked around and figured he must have dug out somewhere and hopefully somebody would call me to come get him. All my dogs are tagged. One of my employees said he found him underneath a shipping container. Somehow this German shepherd had gotten frightened during a night time rainstorm and decided to seek shelter under a 20' steel container. He had dug under it until he was stuck midway. He couldn't back up or turn around. We got a couple shovels and started tunneling under the middle of the structure. We dug down about 2 feet and then under about 4 feet till I had to dig basically with my hands since I was afraid I would hurt the dog with the shovel blade. We also jacked the container up with a car jack just enough to accomplish all this. We finished about noon and my dog Jake scrabbled out covered in mud and shaking. Needless to say he was delighted to see us and promptly went to sleep under my desk in the office.

My point with these stories is they have NOTHING to do with the normal course of business. They are the monsters of risk that just inexplicably show up. All teeth and roaring. You can't ignore them as they may do away with you. So how can you prepare for things like this?

If you are expecting a hard and fast answer, well, I don't have it. Insurance helps. A wealthy family to go crying to would work also. But I mainly keep a cash back up. A cash pad. I've found that when things go wrong, really wrong, and you need money, it's very hard to come by. I stopped letting myself get to that point. A banker who wouldn't loan me a dime taught me this.

This may not be the best way to do things. I mean, it really may be the hard way. That's the way I learned this much of it. Hopefully you reading this will prepare you a bit for the tough days ahead.

Make no mistake. The owners of that abandoned building you are looking at or those closeouts you seek to buy were visited by the very monsters I'm speaking of.

A great many life rules can be learned in a mechanic shop. You learn to follow clues to a hidden solution, you learn to persevere if one method doesn't work and look for other answers. You learn to crank a bolt just far enough that it's tight but not to the point of breaking it. You learn this by touch. You learn to give and take and discover that both need finesse in this world.

What I wish I had learned was how to hire and fire employees. I was terrible at being a boss. I probably should have fired a few of my guys almost immediately instead of feeling sorry for them and keeping them on.

I wound up sabotaging myself due to my inability to get mean when it was necessary.

You may laugh at that. Everybody can be mean! Well sure. But can you be mean when it's necessary, not just because you feel like being mean? What if being mean is the furthest part of your psyche? Can you use it to your best advantage and not run people off? Can that meanness be used as a conscious tool?

From Blogger, Fish and Hickey Bar. "Confrontation"

I hate confrontations. I generally will avoid personal confrontations for as long as I can. My friends will tell you they notice that I simply won't be around certain people. I find it easier to just be over yonder when the aggressor or aggravator is in my locale.

Business, however, is a different matter. Occasionally in business, I'm forced to confront someone or some entity who is strictly out for themselves. Generally at my expense of course.

It took me awhile when I was young to slowly adapt. I was a peacemaker from way back who believed in doing to others as I would have them do to me. This attracted my many customers but left me open for some short sighted, predatory business people. I found after many bruises that always being agreeable isn't the best way to work. Some of those guys looked at me like I was an apple tree. They only want the fruit and they don't care what they have to do to pluck it. Sometimes I'm amazed that DC Mach has survived to this age.

I learned to recognize these particular scumbags and now avoid them if I can in my daily commerce. If a deal surfaces, and it really has value, then the confrontational battle can begin. I have to deal with these less than honorable D--k Heads every so often even now.

Fine.

The trick is being ready for someone who has no interest in your wellbeing whatsoever. It takes a bit of practice for somebody like me while others get right to it with no problem.

So, here is the deal. The vendors I hold close know it. I don't take advantage of them, I don't ask for too many concessions; I bend if they have a shipping problem or a cost issue. Why? Because we are of the same cut. We are the same type of people. I will actively seek out that kind of business person. We should take care of each other as best we can. Any deal we make is mutually beneficial.

What's better than that?

In business, nothing.

But those who try to take instead of trade are now easily seen. I wish I knew this when I started many years ago. It would have saved me a ton of money and grief.

The only advice I can give to newbies and youngsters is to find an older business mentor. It will save you much stress as you go. Or do like I did and figure it out for yourself. I hope you are a bit quicker study than I was though.

There will always be that guy who will walk into your yard to steal your newspaper, or kick your dog if nothing else is handy.

He wants your stuff, plain and simple. He thinks he has power.

Show him your teeth.

I have always been told to treat others as I wished to be treated in return. I found this to be partially untrue. I never need much handholding or needed a boss on my butt to keep me working, so I gave my employees free rein way too often. Just because I shined like that does not mean they can. Most employees can't handle having a lot of freedom to work within. It is only with years of background that I can see now that it was unfair of me to expect them to be more than they were. Sadly, we are not all created equal in the ability to perform. I was totally wrong in thinking it way back then. I blame it on my tendency to introversion too. I have always hated telling someone else what to do. Kind of difficult to build an empire like that, yet, I have.

Years later, another misconception I had about employees was that they actually wanted Christmas parties or that they wanted to be part of the "family" in the business. I set a party up and made it mandatory attendance. I told them we would have the finest steak company money would buy and that I would give everyone their bonus checks. I even had an open bar for them.

They all showed up. I did notice that most seemed to be uncomfortable and wanting to be somewhere else. As we ordered our meals and sat there sipping our drinks, I started a short speech about where the company was and where we were going. You know, like you see company presidents do on TV. My guys were staring at the ceiling, fidgeting, whispering to each other, and basically looking horribly uncomfortable. I cut the story off, gave them their bonus checks and inwardly vowed to never give another party again. My take-away was that they were there for the money, and that was all. The team I thought I had fostered simply didn't exist. A real team would be just as happy having hotdogs and beer at the office as dressing up and going to a restaurant. Obviously, I needed to work on my team building.

I still do parties but I allow the employees to arrange them. That way they are invested in the whole process. After all, it's not all about me, right? It's for us.

Finally, we installed the phone system ourselves, then bought and installed a sign on my building and we were open! Now I just had to make the $550 notes for the next 20 years -

Which I did, and in my memory, on time too. We did pretty well for a self-taught mechanic and a bunch of near outlaws. We worked long hot days and did a lot of non paying warranty work. What I mean by this is that the mechanics were paid but the shop wasn't. I figured the warranty work was more tuition payments in that business and so didn't mind it. I call it all R&D now. I feel like the cost of research and development is practically negligible since it has the power to repay me constantly for my lifetime.

To this day I spend the money.

I actually offered to replace an ac system on a Dodge for free labor, just to learn how to do it. By the end of the job I knew all the necessary steps, the customer got a great deal at cost, and I had a new skill to use the rest of my career. Was I an expert at it? NO. But that bit of "research" paid for itself so many times I lost count. Expertise only comes with repetition, if ever.

My shop lasted for a good long while. Over twenty years, in which my kids grew up and even helped some. I bet to this day my boy Charlie can still fix a tire if he had to. When he joined the military I told him tell no one he could do it. I told him to not let them pigeon hole him into vehicle maintenance. Since he knew what that meant and had seen me come home filthy and covered in grease and oil many times, he was quiet about it his whole career.

In these late days I begin to see more wisdom in protecting your background from those who might use your skills to their best advantage but not necessarily yours.

Finally, things at my business began to change. After all the years of making a small but steady living, I began to lose more money than I made. It was so gradual at first I actually didn't believe it. Then it seemed that every single job had some sort of warranty attached to it. Every job seemed to be extra trouble and developed things that even my experience couldn't help me with. Many of my customers disappeared and never came back. At first it was just a few and that would be normal for any business but toward the end I had constant trouble with every job. I even started doing mechanic work myself to try and turn the trend. I tried to fix a friend's truck air conditioning and absolutely failed to the point that I gave the vehicle back to him with no charge. I probably had 40 hours labor in it and $2000 in parts. It was as if God was saying, "This isn't for you anymore. Time to change." Man, I was a slow learner and so He had to allow me to fail repeatedly before I finally got it. I think I warranted the last 6 or 7 jobs in a row, all with brain draining problems I had never seen in my career. After 25 years, what are the odds of that happening?

During this failure process I became beat down to the point that all I wanted to do was make a little extra money, clean money, money with no warranty or liability issues, but the money just got tighter and tighter and I had to start juggling the balance in my checkbook. It was terribly depressing to even come to work. I actually had to talk myself out of throwing the keys back over the gate as I left one day. I argued that I was still self-employed and that was something so many people wanted and would never get. How ungracious could I be? I simply had to change, like I always had to when I became desperate.

4 ECOMMERCE FOR INTROVERTS

Back in 1997 or 98, I was messing around in the office one day surfing on AOL (remember them?) and landed on eBay. I had heard of it. It didn't look like much. Bunch of people selling junk. I bought something off of it. I remember being so worried about using my credit card online. Everybody knew how dangerous that was! Then, after I bought a couple things, for grins, I figured out how to list an item to just see what would happen. Maybe I could actually sell something the way these people were doing. I can remember it being such a mystery. I wish I could remember what item I sold but the fog of time dims my memory of such things.

I started out of boredom one day because there just wasn't anything I could do to increase business at the shop. Yet almost immediately I could see a glimmer of potential in this eBay thing. I started selling odd things I had around the house. I knew nothing about ecommerce except that it looked so left field and that it just looked like fun and it had nothing to do with people face to face. I was so attracted to the whole concept. I have always been sales oriented so as I made these small sales it hooked me hard. It had what I call now the Whoa Factor.

The Whoa Factor has to do with anything that stops you in your mental tracks for a moment. That tiny moment when you get a glimmer of what an unknown future might look like. It pulls you up short and makes you stare like a tourist. The Whoa Factor is very valuable and can change your future in an instant. Always stop and revel in it as it's like being given far sight or time travel for just a moment. If you don't stop to study it can be gone in an instant as if it were never there in the first place. Consequently, I will never apologize for stopping to stare off into the distance as I study all the previously unknown opportunities. Receiving a Whoa Factor moment is a blessing, make no mistake

But even in these early days, I had so much to learn. The venue was new and it was changing constantly. How to ship these items? I remember being terrified of the post office. They tolerated my questions and terrible packing skills just barely. I remember condescension and impatience. Like everybody who starts this I did everything wrong and I hated facing them with all my mistakes. I always added incorrect shipping fees since I had to guess in advance of a buyer sending me an order. It was a huge stumbling block and one that trips up people even now. With all the time past, I can pretty much guess what shipping costs by now. In fact I'm pretty good at picking up a box and guessing weight. Even to the ounce!

I slowly gained the knowledge of how to sell and make a small profit. It wasn't enough to mention though.

My daughter Cara actually gave me my first true online sales success story. She was a promotions model and has even done her father the generosity of helping me show a few items over the years. She was my model I could never have afforded.

She is one of the few young ladies I've ever met that made her living off her looks and her brain. She figured it out quite young and has managed to support herself all these years and can still do it around taking care of two little boys and a husband.

She occasionally would wind up with premiums at the end of a promotion. They were giveaways. The companies didn't want them and were throwing them away. Sometimes it was little boxes, other times key chains, this time however, she asked me if I wanted a bunch of lanyards.

What's a lanyard?

She told me it was string like a necklace that holds ID for schools or companies. She said I should just pull the advertising off of it and try to sell it on eBay.

I was doubtful, but still game to try it. This was the beginning of my **shotgun approach** to buying merchandise. I will speak of it later.

I wrote my listing, faithfully reading all the instructions EBay had in those days and doing it as clearly as possible. I took many, many photos till they looked somewhat decent and just guessed at what shipping I should specify. All I had was a bathroom scale to weigh my packages. I remember using flash on my camera so the lanyards could really be seen well. LOL. It was only later I discovered flash photography was about the worst thing I could do to a photo. I made my listing public and waited. A couple days later, bam! I sold a set of 30 pieces of lanyards for about $5. Of course my shipping was set too low and I lost money on that. The lanyards though were free so I got that money at least. I set the shipping higher. Plus, I went up on the sale price of the lanyards to $6. I sold another one! This time I discovered that I had to buy manila envelopes so I went up another dollar to offset costs. Now I listed them at $7. I remember worrying that I was pricing them too high. Yet it sold immediately. Being new, I was probably undercutting all other sellers and gaining great search rank by doing so. I certainly didn't know a thing about researching my competition. I wound up selling these lanyards at $9.99 per 30 pc set with $5 shipping. I think I had 300 sets. All my start money came from this wonderful happy accident. Well, not ALL, as I did have an ongoing business but it wasn't doing well and I had no extra funds there at all.

As it was a happy accident I studied what happened from the discovery of the item to the sale and decided to replicate that path as often as possible. Still it took several years to figure it out, if I've ever figured it out.

I not only funded my **cash stash** for this business but also expanded my knowledge of marketing, sourcing and handling. I "sourced" all around my house, neighborhood garage sales and even hit an estate sale or two. I did ok but immediately realized that, for me, sourcing was hard this way. I wanted easier procurement. I eventually stayed totally away from estate sales. Why show up to buy things at a seller's marketplace? Every estate sale I shopped was crowded with people who were buying items with no seeming regard to cost whatsoever. It was a giant waste of time for me. The only thing I found that was routinely a great buy were books at estate sales. It's amazing the books people kept in their personal libraries. I made a lot of money back then selling books. Note that I'm speaking of 'How To' and reference books. I did terrible with fiction and actually threw quite a bit of it away over the years. One great buy was a large set of books on land surveying. Plus it included quite a bit of history that related to it. I made about a thousand bucks off this set that I literally bought for a dollar each.

Cash stash or cash pad is what you have to have behind you. Your savings. Like that old saying, "cash talks, bullsh*t walks". I have had to walk away from many deals because I simply couldn't afford them. Having the cash available is one of the most powerful feelings in business. When all you have to do is say, yes or no, and not worry about 'can I afford this?' Start a company savings as soon as you can. Start small. I actually started at $1 a day. I'm not kidding, but I built my cash stash from that and still add to it to this day. It's such a habit now I don't even notice. It's some of the best insurance I've ever bought and paid for.

I actually lived off credit cards for a while and even financed some of my mechanic shop with them. I would sign up for a card with free interest and then switch to another when the grace period was about to run out. If you have to go this way, I do understand, but you understand that your risk is ratcheted up quite a bit. If something happens, and it always seems to, you may not be able to pay your cards back as promptly as you hoped.   Then, you've got more debt to deal with.   Just use cards as sparingly as you can for investment purposes.

A way I use credit cards to this day is for the rewards they offer.   It's hard to pass up the 1 or 2% cash back or loads of airline miles.   Again, I urge you to pay these off monthly, and if you can use them very sparingly as they can get the better of your money so quickly.

I continued to look for other items.   I even tried to sell other people's stuff for a percentage and soon discovered it was too much trouble and they never wanted to agree to the split. The deal always went sideways when I was splitting the money, no matter what we agreed to at first.   I just stopped doing it.   In those days I charged 30% plus shipping fees.   I finally changed it to 50% and I covered all shipping.   It was a bust and another avenue that just didn't work out.   One reason it was a bust was the tremendous amount of time I had to spend just talking to the person selling the item.   When you work alone you begin to dodge **time suckers** like that.   I found that some of these people actually watched the listing all day and would call to let me know when someone bid on it................. It was killing me!   I even had a few who decided right in the middle of an auction they didn't want to sell (because the price was too low) and demanded I cancel it.   I had enough of that pain.

Once during all this I decided to make some Hog Traps.   Remember that I was pretty crafty and had a welder and cutting torch.   I also hunted on a lease not far from my shop.   I built several traps and took them out and tested them.   They definitely caught wild hogs so somehow during all this I became the resident hog catching expert. What I didn't expect was to become the home place of hopeful hog hunters or more **time suckers**. These guys would come by my shop and just hang out and follow me around talking about all the hogs they had trapped, were going to trap, or hoped to learn to trap. Sometimes I would have 3 or 4 of them. It became so maddening that I actually tried my best to stay away from them. (My introvert self showing up?). Finally, I sold the last trap and swore off them. I literally let my extra steel material grow into the trees on the fence line. It's a monument to **time suckers** and a reminder to steer clear of them.

Note that my reactions to these time suckers might be more of the traits of an introvert than I ever thought previously. I honestly didn't like the interaction and generally couldn't wait till the buyers were gone. Probably not the healthiest way to deal with customers. That's why the ecommerce world has saved me so much grief.

During all this ecommerce schooling I was fortunate to find an eBay message board with a lot of good advice. Don't ask a dumb question though or they could be pretty mean. Something happened and they split up later on. The IMA (Internet Merchants Association) was formed right after that by old buddies and mentors, Tom and Steve. Without the advice of these guys who were pioneers at this type of business, I doubt I would be here now.

I met both on the message boards and met them in person in Las Vegas at the ASD show. One of my fav quotes comes from Steve. **"Do things that make money, stop doing things that don't make money."**

Simple as that.

Money was so very tight in those days that experimental purchases had great risk attached. I felt that I had to protect my company and employees. My success was their success, but so too my failure would hurt them. My failure could very well be their lost job. I began to feel desperate again. This is when I began to pray before my trips and sometimes right in the middle of an isle at the show. I needed help and guidance badly and didn't feel I was "smart" enough to even be doing this type of work.

As for asking a trusted associate? Well, there just weren't very many of us. We were all feeling our way forward in the dark. One person's method was different from another person's so who is to say which one was right? Honestly I just didn't trust very many people to know much more than I did.

What I didn't have in smarts and background, I made up in dogged persistence. My motivation was my children, my employees, my ex and my wife. Buy low and sell high was just a natural viewpoint for me though I didn't know it exactly. There was no good way to search eBay for sales history at first. I actually carried a 10 lb. laptop in case I had a chance to do some searches. Sales people hated that I took photos of their product. I was normally pretty sneaky about it but occasionally had to defend myself. I explained that otherwise I couldn't remember what I saw that day. While that was true, I mainly used the photos to hunt for other people selling these items. UPC codes weren't used early on so that didn't do me any good.

I bought all kinds of experimental stuff at the shows. One of my "hits" was a little ceramic coffee grinder. It was beautiful. I got a great price for it too, only problem is that it didn't work very well. The little knob would fall off when the handle was turned and every grinder had to be taken apart and adjusted so it would actually grind coffee. And even then it was coarse grind only.

I think I bought these units at $2.5 each and sold them, not including shipping, for $19.99. We wound up with a lot of labor in them but at least it wasn't a loss.

Then I found a guy wholesaling plastic fish. Large plastic fish. Few other people wanted to sell something as large as these were so I had the market to myself for a long time. Even then I was looking for items that fit the Blue Ocean strategy. Average sell price was about $35 each. This was my beginning moment of selling stuff that other people simply couldn't get or didn't want to sell. There is safety in selling stuff that others didn't have or couldn't have. All I knew was to avoid competition as much as I could. They were all bigger than me, had more money than me, and knew more than me, so my saving instinct was to avoid them.

I went through many "hits" as I called them and many misses but I developed a system of buying and reselling that has stuck with me all through.

After I had become relatively established, meaning that I had consistent sales, I began to realize my system was valuable. I had somehow stumbled on one of my primary objectives for buying. First buy things other people don't sell. When a bunch of sellers gang up on an item, the price falls.   Most of the sellers get hurt in this.   At the end though when everybody is out of this item, you can get the margin you need.   I have waited a year on several items that were down in the dumps selling for pennies more than I paid for it when then all the other sellers finally ran out and I could slowly raise the price up to a profitable level.

Yah, waiting that long stinks and you got to have all kinds of storage facilities.   Then you have to worry about the item going bad before you can sell it.   In my case the heat is terrible in Texas and will ruin some items if left in storage too long.   Also, it's humid here on the coast.   If something can rot it will.   Then occasionally termites or wood eating ants get in your cardboard boxes and have a party.   Not to mention rats and mice also needing homes. So, slowly, I began to develop rules about the type of items I could carry.

So, this is it.

I will admit in advance that this may not be the best way to do things but it is the way I felt safest making the attempt.   If I failed I would have suffered the smallest loss possible.   If I succeeded I made enough to buy more and bigger inventory to keep it all going forward.   I remember when I prayed for 3 or 4 sales a day.   That's all I wanted.   It's was a lofty goal in those days.   Ten sales a day was success.   20 sales a day was dreamland.   LOL, now 100 plus is the norm and I'm only one of thousands doing this, many light years larger and hopefully smarter too.

5 WORKING IT

First things first.

Learn to buy on the Internet. If you have read from the beginning, this may sound odd, but learning to buy is as important as learning to sell. Actually make some purchases on the market you want to sell on. Learn to shop and do research on the different platforms. It's important that you are an expert buyer. Amazon is different from EBay who is different from Etsy who differs from Wal-Mart. This may sound simplistic but I have found people for years now who want in this business but don't actually buy much on the Internet. They have all kinds of excuses for it from "I'm not really computer literate", to, "I don't trust putting my credit card and info out there," or "I don't want people knowing my business!"

Note that as time moves forward I think it would be rare now to find a person that doesn't buy on the Internet. Learning to buy smart though, still takes time.

As for the different platforms, to say that one is better than the other is just plain lazy. Each platform has its strong points. Amazon is the giant of the woods having actually trained its customers to come to them first, while EBay has a tendency to sell the odd and one of a kind though they have really leaned towards bringing the Chinese sellers into the market. Etsy has a ton of one of a kind, handmade items that are also hard to find anywhere but there. Wal-Mart, while another giant in the woods is still learning the ropes. They tend to push the cheapest of the cheap. Not to say they only sell junk, they don't, but they seem to place pricing consideration over everything else. Consider what you are selling and where it will do the most good. After a while, if you persist, you might wind up selling on all of them anyway.

Once you have learned how to buy on the Internet and where to go to save the most money, and where to go to find the best deals on a particular item, only now is it time to learn to sell on it.

I say this so you begin to learn what you want as a buyer from a seller on the Internet. You will never meet the person selling the item. You are going by faith. You build your faith as a buyer with experience. This experience is helped by your trust in the platform. Most all platforms will protect your purchase as a buyer and should you be unhappy with your purchase, help you return the item to get your money back. You will learn to appreciate speedy shipping. Further you will appreciate free shipping.

Eventually you will learn to appreciate a good warranty issued by the seller or the platform. An easy returns process is also a plus. Not everything you buy online will be perfect for you. Sending it back can be a big pain sometimes. It's the nature of the Internet.

So, you have become versed and experienced as an online buyer. Now you are thinking, hey maybe I want to try this. Let's sell something!

But what to sell? First, I looked all over my house for things to sell. Then I looked to EBay as the best place to sell second hand or used items. How do I know this? By experience. In the beginning Amazon wasn't around. While they try, Amazon doesn't really do used items or antiques or one-of-a-kind unusual things. They may have dipped a toe in it but historically they ignored it. EBay has been maddeningly slow in embracing that strength. The actuality is that it's a huge strength for them. At one time literally anything you could think of was for sale on EBay. That has slacked off in recent days but it is still my go to place for oddities, parts, used, and one of a kind, (OOAK) items.

Thankfully, I was talked into making a trip to Las Vegas to see the ASD show. I was told it stood for the Association of Specialty Discounters (which was totally wrong even if appropriate) and it was also my first visit with the Internet Merchants Association.

The ASD is a huge wholesale show with just about everything under the sun for sale. It's vast, and to see all of it takes several days.

I was terrified of failure on that trip too. I had very little money with which to try and find inventory. I couldn't bear any mistakes. I have since learned to survive even through bad purchases.

One thing that helped in those wild days was developing a network of Ecommerce buddies. It's pretty important for long term business development. What I mean is that the problems you confront may have previously been solved by somebody else. They can give you a lot of help in certain situations. You won't have to reinvent the wheel. Now you can develop this circle of buddies, confidants, and mentors on Facebook. I'm sure you can do it on other services too but Facebook is where I landed and pretty much stay. I currently belong to about 10 groups there. Some as large as 16k members, and some as small as 8. Just about any question I need answered can be or can be referred. I cannot overemphasize the amount of expertise that lives in these groups. Become a member and soak up that hard fought for knowledge that they will so generously give to you. **Ask and you will receive.**

Since I didn't know what would sell I tried my best to purchase the smallest amount of an item possible, though the wholesalers don't really like that. Generally all the wholesalers will have some kind of minimum purchase requirement from a single case to a single pallet. Some even have dollar minimums. It can be from a few hundred dollars to the largest I remember was $10,000.00. Needless to say I walked out of their booth.

This spending on merchandise can get dangerous quickly. Unless you are cash flush with a huge cash stash, don't let the wholesaler tell you how much you are going to spend. In fact, never let the wholesaler do that. They ALWAYS want you to spend more than you have.

This is where I developed the **shotgun approach** to purchasing. Where you buy small amounts of individual SKUs (Stock Keeping Unit) to test which items will sell. Just put them up for sale and see what happens. These tests are very inexpensive research and development. If you find yourself with a dud it's a lot easier to liquidate a single case in comparison to a full pallet of duds. I actually began to call them test pallets. I still have salespeople ask if I want to build one out of their merchandise. Since I don't really know which items will sell I buy as many SKUs as possible that will fit in my small purchase. Note that after a while my smallest purchase was a pallet so I could get lots of different items on it. My risk of buying a dud is lessened but most importantly the opportunity to find a hit increases tremendously.

Just in case you are thinking I randomly start picking items and telling the sales guys to write them up; I don't. I have a system that utilizes what I call the **Whoa factor**. If the item doesn't have that, I won't hardly buy it. It has to strike my imagination, or provide a perfect fix for a problem, or just be cool. Whatever cool is.

I would imagine As Seen On TV uses something like this when they scout for items. So many of their items have the whoa factor. Some things just grab you the moment you see them. You can feel that an item might work. I imagine that I will get a lot of flack about using my emotion as a gauge on what I buy and what I don't. But I have history and a proven record of being able to find that WHOA factor item. I will admit that what makes me say WHOA might not translate to you.

For instance, I was digging around in junk bins under a table at a booth when I found a giant safety pin made of stainless steel. WHOA, what's this? This thing was 5" long and made for industrial use. I asked the salesman how many in a minimum order and he said one case which was 500 pieces. I almost walked away. So I looked on EBay and Amazon and Google right quick to see if anyone was selling something like this. I found one person selling through Google Shopping. It began to look a little better to me so I said send me a case. I don't remember what else I bought there since everything else paled to this WHOA item. When I got back to my shop I decided to sell these in sets of 10. I started them on EBay and they slowly started to sell. I then listed them on Amazon and the sales picked up and got pretty steady. Several a day. As I sold through my stock I reordered 5000 more pieces. Sales actually picked up even further and I bought all the guy had. About 10,000 pieces. Finally I found another vendor with stock and I bought 100,000 pieces. Yes this was a definite hit. Somehow crafters loved the things and I made good money off them. Cost about $1.50 each set. Retailed between $10.99 to $15.99 per set. I tried and tried to find a manufacturer in China to make them for me but I couldn't get a good price to make it worthwhile.

Remember, sometimes even the WHOA factor won't keep me from buying a dud. You have to be prepared even when an item looks like a sure thing to eat it. I bought some beautiful bathroom scales that were so rare online there just wasn't any. I bought a small quantity.

When I got home I listed them and they flew off the shelf. I called my vendor and bought an entire pallet. By the time they arrived I noticed my sales had started slowing down. I did a little research and found that all of a sudden I had 20 competitors and sure enough they were already price fighting. Soon the price fell to the floor and I had to liquidate to try and get my money back. I think I still got a couple lying around someplace. I now use them as charity donations for silent auctions.

Remember to ask your vendor how much stock they have and who is selling it other than them. You need to know if somebody is about to dump 200,000 units on the market. Most likely I wouldn't have enough money to buy the entire stock out, so I might elect to sit that item out. Sometimes I bought an item that just looked great (and priced right) no matter that it had crazy competition. I put it aside and waited till the competitors ran out of stock. I once waited a year. Doing the research will let you know how to proceed to make a good purchase. Believe me, if I didn't have the cash I would never buy something that would take a year to sell. In fact, I don't recommend it as a method, but it happens anyway.

Finding that elusive hit is the coolest thing of my business life. I do love the hunt to this day.

One of my absolute first items sold online was a small aluminum propeller for an antique boat motor. I took the picture (badly, I'm sure) and I don't remember how much I sold it for. It doesn't matter. I had found it in my Dad's shop at his lake house. No telling how old it was. The wonderful platform that is EBay connected me with a buyer from who knows where.

Ta Dah!   I was successful!

I tried several times to get my Dad interested in selling stuff online as he was very fortunate in always finding great potential merchandise.   In his later years he had this very interesting job as a retiree gate keeper for a garbage dump.   Now this wasn't just any old garbage dump, but a wealthy people's dump.   He was bringing home wonderful finds.   I sold them and told him how much I was making. He was tickled but not interested in selling.   My Dad could never see himself as any kind of salesman.   I think that's why he was always mystified by me.   I could always figure a way to turn things into money.

Then there were books. I've always loved books and have a collection of beloved finds from over the years.   It was only natural that I went that direction.   Soon I began to sell used books and had a tremendous number of almost keepers in my library. I didn't make much on them but now that I look back that didn't matter.   I was learning to sell. As for the books themselves, I then learned to grade and describe their condition so that my buyers weren't surprised when they received them.   Then I was learning to pack. Then I learned to ship.   Also during this I learned to say pleasant things to my buyers.   Thanks for buying my item. I will ship it at the first opportunity. You should get it by such and such date.   The market was pretty good and I made great money.

Sometime during this sales season several huge booksellers showed up on eBay and started selling books for 99 cents at auction. They didn't care what kind of book either.   These guys absolutely destroyed the book market. In the end when I couldn't sell them or even give them away, I literally threw wheel barrows of books in the dumpster. Seriously traumatic for a book lover, but I still kept my personal collection and continue to add to it when I can. I got some great books and will let my kids worry about getting rid of them someday.

I mentioned garage sales. I would drive all over on Saturdays and buy whatever I felt like I could gamble on. Everything was a gamble in those days. Note that the sense of gambling decreases with experience gained. When I knew practically nothing about this business I did tend to buy all kinds of things that I got stuck with. Duds. Part of the process you have to learn is to sell/get rid of things that are ummm, hard to sell. (or near impossible) You will hate the effort it takes getting that stuff out of your house or garage so that it will immediately make you a better buyer. As time goes you won't make those bad purchases as often. You will still take risks in the future but you will control the risk so much better. I hadn't totally formed my Whoa Factor yet, but it was coming.

Selling items that aren't necessarily wanted by a lot of people is tough. However learning to do it is a requirement in this business. You will make mistakes all the time but recovering from those mistakes is what makes you a business person that will last.

Note, easy selling days don't make you as tough and resilient as the hard selling days, so expect them, learn from them and deal with them to your advantage as much as possible. You will find ways and procedures that will help you survive later on. Is it painful? Yes it's painful, and the pain makes you naturally avoid it.

Learning how to deal with your customers.....

Dealing well with customers can not only save you a lot of money but it can make you lifetime customers that come back again and again. Plus you can soothe a lot of misunderstandings or bad descriptions by just being polite and considerate. Misunderstandings are going to happen. I rewrite listings all the time trying my best to clarify an issue to keep future customers from emailing me questions. I suggest you go the extra mile in some manner that doesn't cost you a small fortune. Try to set yourself apart from your competitors. Way back, I knew sellers who included freebies in a box like a nice handwritten note card or a small gadget or even a stick of chewing gum. All these things were designed to show appreciation but also as a small way of smoothing ruffled feathers - in advance.

Sometimes showing appreciation can backfire. Years ago I was a route salesman in the oilfield. On a weekly basis, I would go by warehouses and fill their shelves with our items. This was a competitive business since other salespeople could stock their products right by mine. While visiting with an old customer over lunch he mentioned that in his youth salesmen would include a free gift of candy, or gum, or a small toy in the boxes. It was just a small and inexpensive way to get the customers to choose your box to open because it came with a prize. Kind of like Cracker Jacks.

I thought that was great. I bought a bunch of gum and stuck a stick in every box that I stocked in the warehouse. After a few weeks, I noticed nothing. No sales increase, no notice of any kind from the customers. So, I raised the stakes a little and placed a dollar in each box. My commission covered this easily. After one week I showed up and discovered that YES my sales had increased. It worked! I continued adding a dollar to the inventory and anxiously showed back up the following week to count the inventory that sold. As I pulled into the parking lot I noticed the big door to the warehouse was wide open. There was also a mountain of torn cardboard boxes laying everywhere. I looked at my inventory and noticed that it was all gone off the shelves and now laid out on the floor everywhere with no boxes. The warehouse manager came up to me.

"Somebody broke in. We don't know how much was stolen. I need you to pick up all your stuff and count it to see what's missing."

Surprisingly, none of my stuff was missing, except of course, for the dollar bill I had placed in each box. I didn't mention that little experiment to my customer. Not all sales gimmicks work and most should be judiciously tested. You never know what the unintended consequences might be.

As you find items to sell, you begin to learn how to write a really strong listing. It's amazing to me to read listings on eBay that are basically a picture, price, and that's it. I wonder if anyone actually buys things like that? I suppose they do. I answer questions almost daily concerning minute issues with my items. I always list the weight, sizes, colors. If I didn't have all that in my listings the questions would be constant or worse the buyers would simply ignore my wares.

When I say write a strong listing, I mean, write good marketing. For instance, if you are selling buckets, don't sell the little metal round thing with a hole in one end and a handle on top. Instead, sell a great little utility bucket for garden or yard work. Perfect for seedlings and on up to larger plants. Bottom can be easily pierced for better drainage. Attractive galvanized finish for long life and perfect for shabby chic arrangements to country decor. Even works as flower arrangement pots for weddings and other gatherings. These little buckets are cute and totally usable for your next project.

Then follow this great writing with great pics of buckets with flowers in them, sit them on steps, on tables, on mantles, and anywhere else. Even have a model holding them. Show the buckets being used in real life.

When pricing, use the amount that is the most reasonable. Sometimes when you start out on a platform it will take awhile for search to work for you. I very rarely advertise a new item but wait to see how it will fare organically. It may take 2 or 3 weeks to see. Sometimes I don't have to do a thing and the item just takes off. Other times I change the price all over or advertise on Amazon or Google.

You never know what effect your item will have when finally received by a buyer. What you see and understand about this won't be what the buyer will feel when he gets it. You will learn to constantly edit your listings as you try to clarify every single thing in your offer. You want your listing **bump free**. I don't want that buyer asking me a question that I could have answered before hand.

Note, ANYTHING that causes a hitch, or bump, or hesitation needs to be removed from a listing. Everything in it should guide the buyer to the "add to cart" button. Nothing should stop this! Go through the listings and take out anything that might interrupt the flow. Further, add things that help direct the buyer.

Another very important thing is to make the buying process as smooth and bump free as possible. I read others listings all the time and am always surprised when reading titles and descriptions of even long time sellers who leave all kinds of questions unanswered. Size, color, quantity are basic. Weight should be included too. Don't make the buyer doubt his future purchase! Don't make them send you an email asking something that you should have included in the original description.

I'm finding myself repeating this bump free condition in a listing. This carries over to how your website works too. I will speak of this later. It's incredibly important to make the buying process as smooth and friction free as possible. No bumps!

It wasn't too long before I figured out that selling one item at a time, while fun and profitable, wasn't really enough to sustain me and make for a stable business. I began to look for quantities of items. I still didn't have much money but I bought what I could.

6 CONTINUING EDUCATION (OR ALL THE OTHER STUFF THEY DIDN'T TELL YOU ABOUT)

Are you a photographer?   No?   You will be.

Don't get all flustered. Get a camera, any kind of camera.   A modern cell phone takes pretty good pictures that are plenty good enough for Internet sales.   Take a lot of pictures of your item from every angle using all kinds of light.   Don't use a flash!   It makes the pictures look amateurish.   I use natural light as much as I can even though I now have a photo booth that is fully lighted to help speed the photo process.   This might sound weird but I like overcast days to take pictures outside.   Those days make your colors pop somehow. Take the pic of your item on a plain white or blue, or tan background.   You may have to experiment to see which way your item looks best.   Another thing I like to do is include the item with another common item that others know the size of at a glance. For instance many of my buckets were posed with a coffee cup. Knowing the size of a coffee cup gives a buyer an instant idea of what size the bucket is. You will probably have to remark that the items don't come with the cup, because someone somewhere will ask about it. I also pose my buckets with flowers that can show the size of the bucket at a glance. I further urge you to post several pictures of your item on the listing. That way the buyer won't have to ask any questions thereby slowing down the sale.

I know that some sites insist on a white background for your pictures. You can learn Photoshop which has a pretty good learning curve or hire an outside service to do it, or do it yourself with a free program from Bonanza called Background Burner. It's what I use and works pretty well, and it's free. The only note I will include here is to give it time to work. I found it to be relatively slow but it does work. Check my pics out on my site. They look pretty good. However, just because you got one killer pic on a white background does not let you off the hook. Take more shots to get other angles or with other objects or with a human being using it. More pictures mean more acceptance and less questions.

A further note on pictures. This is equal in importance to the title of your item. While your title allows your item to be found in search the easiest, the picture attracts the eye of the shopper and in many cases cements the deal immediately. Look around in magazines and circulars and study the shots that grab you immediately. What did they do to make that happen? Study it, figure it out, and emulate it. It's not the easiest thing but you got to try to get that level of interest working in your product.   I work at it all the time and still miss more often than not.

Note that the future of shopping includes picture search (not just word search), so again, I can't over emphasize the importance of a great picture. (Or series of pictures)   I know you are saying 'but I'm not a photographer.'   Don't worry, if you persist in this business, you will be.   It comes to you, so don't quit.   Digital pictures are relatively free compared to what they used to be.   We had to get them developed and then wait a few days to see what a terrible photographer we were.   Nowadays you can learn how terrible you are instantly.   The joy of technology!

More notes.   I'm taking nothing from professional photographers.   Their training far surpasses any effort I've made to learn to take a pic for internet presentation.   If you can afford a pro then hire a pro.   I couldn't afford one at first, but I've hired several since.   Make sure they give you complete rights to the picture though.   Some photographers think they are Michelangelo and insist they own the pic forever.   That's bull!   You pay them for their work, they aren't creating art, they are creating a likeness for mass ecommerce consumption and an industrial picture that will be stolen and used all over the Internet.   Use your judgment on this but insist that if you are paying them, you own the pic unconditionally.   If they disagree, then move on to the next one.   I hate the thought of a photographer hitting me up one day wanting royalties for a catalog pic they took way back.

Speaking of education, I've always been a reader.   I learned early on that if you want cheap entertainment, books couldn't hardly be beat and while I have been a huge science fiction reader almost all my reading life, I also read self help books. I mentioned the Time Life books earlier but I went further than that and began to ask for recommendations later on. I wish I could remember all those people but my memory isn't that great. One of the first business books I ever read was "Why SOBS Succeed And Nice Guys Fail In A Small Business." An eye opening view of big business real estate deals. It read like tooth and nail battle. I'm not sure I ever followed the advice in it but it made me aware of those types of people and how to recognize them as quickly as possible. Then I just avoid them as much as I can. I don't need, nor want to do business that way. I've found that it just isn't necessary to be a snatch and plunder type business person. I'm not saying I haven't resorted to it in the past but utilizing that strategy day in and day out isn't for me.

Here are a few other books I loved for business.

The E Myth revisited: Why Most Small Businesses Don't Work and What to Do about It.

Art & Money by Julia Trops. (A hard eyed view of art and the work it takes to succeed).

Blue Ocean Strategy as recommended by my friend Brandon Dupsky. He and I were talking at one of the Vegas meets when I was describing my business and my philosophy when he stopped me and said I was using the Blue Ocean Strategy. I had never heard of it. Sure enough, it spelled out my direction to a T and actually gave me words for what I was just feeling before. Highly recommended.

The Unlikely Entrepreneur (How I Transformed $100 Into A Seven Figure Business) by Robyn Johnson.

Why Should Anyone Be Led By You? (What It Takes To Be an Authentic Leader)

Kick Ass Social Commerce for E-preneurs by John Lawson. (It's Not About Likes, It's About Sales)

While I will state the amount of great info in these books is invaluable, I'm not vouching for the readability of any of them; and that's my fault. I'm really bad about hunting around in a self-help book to find the good part. I know, that's not the smartest way to read, but I'm generally in a hurry. Remember those bad life choices I mentioned earlier? Yeah, it's why I can't hardly bear to watch a teaching video. They drag so slooooooowwwly.

Learning to Teach Yourself

Luckily, I cultivated an attitude within myself of mutual satisfaction with my customers. It was the hippy- free- love- flower- child within me that hung on from the old days. Whatever deal I wanted to complete I tried to make sure we both benefited from it. As a gesture, I generally made sure my partner would wind up with the extra dollar. That was positive reinforcement that I hoped would bode well for the next transaction, if any. I've always tried my best to develop that kind of good attitude.

Speaking of good positive attitude, I once went to an Art Linkletter conference of positive thinkers and listened to all kinds of speakers. These guys were great and very funny and uplifting but, at the end of it I found that I couldn't quite grasp a positive attitude that overlooked all the realities of life. A LOT of things are placed in our way. We are NOT necessarily supposed to overcome them with nice little butterfly thoughts. I wound up avoiding most positive thinking seminars from that point on. They just seemed crazy to me.

I can't ignore all the thieves, pitfalls, carney barkers, robbers, takers, and the self-righteous A-Holes that I have run into. They really are everywhere. A buddy told me I was paranoid for no reason, right before he left me to founder for myself in a business deal. A scumbag is always ready to take you for a penny or $10k. It's almost no matter to them.

Years ago, when I was running the mechanic shop, I had a guy come by and pick up my scrap iron. It wasn't a bad deal as it kept my place clean of junk that had a tendency to build up. I would even save stuff for him and I refused to give it away to the copycats that came by. Scrappers are notorious and will steal customers from each other in the blink of an eye. Even if they are kin to each other.

My man's name was Charlie and I gave him scrap for several years. He went to jail in the middle of that time and I actually saved the scrap for him till he got out. He was appropriately thankful. We had a pretty good business relationship.

One day he asked if he could borrow my 14' trailer to move some scrap for pay. I told him that since he had been a good hand all these years that yes, I would loan it to him, with warnings to not hurt it. He said he would be back with it the next day.

After three days of many phone calls, he showed up and offered immense apologies. The job was bigger than he expected. The trailer was loaded to the sky, but not with metal scrap, it was loaded with roofing shingles. He apologized for that too and said he would be back over tomorrow to take it to the dump and get rid of it. Sorry for the delay, so sorry.

I didn't see him for a year. He had found a job that paid him to get rid of the shingles and simply dumped them on me. I finally paid to have them towed off and thrown in a county trash dump. It was another lesson, but it really wasn't about trust. I still trust who I will. It was a lesson about money. We don't all value money the same. To him that bit of money he made was worth every possible future loss, if he even thought that far forward.

He came back to me the following fall and asked if he could start picking up my scrap again. I told him that now I could never help him like that since he took advantage of my charity. He smiled like he expected that answer but hoped for something else.

I was a mark that he kind of liked. A flower child that finally wised up.

———————————— more education

Some education is absolutely free and you can get a ton of it off YouTube. Just query the opening page and start listening to all the gurus that post info about selling online there. There is a ton of information. Caution though is warranted. Use your own judgment about who you believe. Some charge a LOT of money for their "course" or club, or mentor group, sometimes calling it a mastermind group. Whatever, they call it, move forward carefully. Read everything you can find and realize that not all of it applies to you.

An education of failures

A further note about education needs to be stated here. Some, if not most of it, will cost you money. One way or another you are going to pay. I tended to pay a lot for my failures and found that they were indeed my tuition for this business. Failing is just a fact of doing business. Hopefully, you fail forward to the next experience. I would imagine it's like learning to do gymnastics. Failing means you hit the floor. But educated failing means you hit the floor softly so you can get back up and try again. Never let yourself get situated to where a failure shuts you down totally. Sticking your neck out too far on a deal can be a speedy yet dangerous way to do things. Always remember the safety of baby steps. **Taking those small steps into the unknown is way better than just stepping off a cliff.**

You could also pay a guru to teach you how to do it, one who literally holds your hand and walks you down the vendor aisles. As funny as that sounds it could save you a lot of money and time and frustration. I was a hard head and had to do things the hard way. My way. Sometimes I can't believe I survived through it. Plus I was actually too poor to pay anybody for anything when I first started. I had to do it myself as an economic necessity. With hindsight, I'm not sure how many gurus were around in those early days. There had to be a couple I would think. Now, however, there are a LOT, so choose carefully if you decide to go that way.

A network of buddies is a great way to find education. Without a network of business buddies you will find that this business is pretty lonely.   There just aren't that many people doing it.   I will go to a Meetup here in Houston occasionally and even that is thinly attended. My membership in the IMA (Internet Merchants Association) certainly kept me alive in this business.   I could tell these people about everything I did wrong and they instantly came up with an solution.   They even, in a weak moment, made me an officer of the organization.   Secretary! I asked if the job came with a badge and a gun and received no answer to my query.   I was immediately placed in charge of bartending duty at our spring and fall meetings and have faithfully performed that duty for years.   I actually speak in a question and answer session at the free education classes.   I'm not sure if I'm there for what I know or for comic relief.

I do try to add as much as I can to our educational mission but have less and less time now.   I will forever be thankful to the IMA board of directors and as many members as I've been fortunate enough to meet.

Group mind is a powerful thing and especially when it's on your side.

I also learned to do my own books.   I've never been scared of numbers so figuring what I was making and what I was spending was pretty easy.   However, later on, keeping track of inventory began to get difficult.   I used excel and slowly, if not painfully, learned some formulas.   I will admit I don't know much more than addition and subtraction and how to add a column of numbers, but I just happened to have some buddies who are spreadsheet masters, and they helped me set up some forecasting pages.

Now, I keep a live inventory that we update every day and sometimes several times a day. I can forecast how many items were sold per week for any number of weeks up to a year. It makes reordering tremendously easier.

As I learned my lessons, I started attempting to scale larger. I immediately ran into the impasse bottleneck of writing listings. I could only write so many and they took a lot of time. Finally, I figured out that if I wrote one listing for 20 identical items instead of writing 20 individual listings things began to pick up. I bought some children's camping tents at a show. A couple cases at first and then 6 cases, and finally entire pallets. I bought some laser level tool kits with the same success. I bought a bunch of baskets once, and then a bunch of hand crosses. As my successes came so did my cash. I found myself able to buy larger quantities. Still, I ran into the next lesson of my buying education.

7 SOME THINGS DON'T SELL OR THE LIST OF SHAME.........

Things change.   Just as I had begun to find some stability in my income and actually spent less than what I made I discovered that I had attained that first small plateau of success.   I was thrilled.   Thankfully I had set my goals low enough to attain them if I didn't mess up horribly. What I didn't consider was that my success was also my manufacturer's success.   With success comes expansion it seems.   As I made a manufacturer more and more money, they would go to tremendous effort to find other sellers just like me.   They would sell to them thinking they were growing their business.   They would even use my success as an advertising tool!   (I actually found one manufacturer using my pictures off of Amazon on his worldwide website.) However, we sellers were all fishing in the same pond so to speak.   More and more sellers were created yet the amount of fish (buyers) remained the same.   We began to fight over these few fish and soon the prices would go down till no one was making any money.   I have walked away from many lines of products over the years.   Not because they weren't good sellers, but because I couldn't make any money selling them at the current prices.   I go back and check on these products every so often and find that most just disappear into nothingness because their market collapsed. This can really happen when some overseas manufacturers jump into the US market with copies.   Whatever value there was for the product just evaporates due to price fighting. Then, and it never fails, the quality of the item begins to go down as the Chinese (or other country) starts cutting back to make more money.   Finally, one more way the product disappears is that we buyers lose faith in it as a profitable item.   We get a bad taste in our collective mouths and just shy away from it whenever we see it.   This can be seen on EBay sometimes when you find an item that's $1.99 and free shipping.   Sounds impossible doesn't it?   It's not.   A year or two and maybe the market straightens itself out.   It's another gamble that should be taken very carefully in case the market is ruined and won't come back.   There is another bad thing that can happen to an item that was once a powerhouse seller.   It can lose momentum.   If that happens you have to start over from scratch as if the item was never sold before.   It can take months to get it back to any semblance of its normal selling self.

In spite of my careful testing for the Whoa Factor and buying in small quantities, I still began to see that some merchandise just did not fit my buying and selling strategy.

For instance, clothing.   Me and clothing have never hit it off.   Everything I ever bought sat in my warehouse to the point that I either gave it away or threw it away as it rotted. I failed with shirts, bed covers, rugs, coffee bean sacks, and even purses. Luckily, since there is so much more merchandise to buy I've never really studied why I can't seem to sell things made of thread. All I know is that failure after failure makes an impression on even me after a while. I avoid that stuff now. Maybe you can sell it though. Maybe that is where your expertise or passion is. Go for it, but do it with all the judgment you can muster.

Another item that seemed to take root and stay at my warehouse was anything to do with professional sports. I know other sellers who sell plenty of that stuff like jerseys, team signs and plaques, coffee mugs, etc. Not me though. Every time I took a chance and bought some I got stuck with it. I have a set of sports cards (cases) that I have had so long I began to donate them to any charity that came up. At least there is some good to come from them. Another item that I won't even consider even to this day. One of my problems with this type of line is that I don't follow sports and so have no basis in what is valuable or not. My original WHOA factor did not help me with this stuff at all. It seemed like I was always wrong about whatever I bought to resell.

A note here about choosing items to resell. Buying things totally out of your experience is just not a good idea. It can be done and a lot of folks do it but the risk is higher. Whenever I began to reach out of my circle of experience was when I got into trouble. My Whoa Factor couldn't help me with items that seemed new and cool to me but we're really lame to those in the know.

Candles. Back when I bought my first small load of candles I was excited about the prospects of selling them.

After all, I knew people who had dozens of candles and routinely burned them every day. They also loved having a variety. What a great item! Plus they have to be replaced so often. A perfect market!

Only one problem got in the way of this financial windfall. The Texas heat. A warehouse that gets to be 108 in the summer isn't conducive to keeping candles in anything but a near liquid state. My load slumped into their selves and formed a kind of candle mass that I chunked into the dumpster. Even then I had to wait till the first northern for the mass to congeal enough to be able to move it.

Note to self. Don't buy/sell candles or anything else that can melt and be worthless.

The story of the screaming chickens.

While hunting up and down the aisles at the ASD show, I found the oddest little creature-doll. It was a chicken made with soft cuddly fur. The interesting part that set my Whoa Factor meter running was that this chicken was made to be a sling shot. The legs were rubber. Hold the head, pull back on the legs, let go, and the thing flew across the room. What really got me going was that the chicken made a sound like one of those rubber chickens and was really funny to listen to as it soared through the air. After checking online, none showing, I bought 100 of them.

When I received them at my shop in Houston, my guys were amazed. We shot the screaming chickens all over and laughed and laughed. All of us were convinced we were going to sell a lot of these little toys. That night we left the case open sitting in the middle of the shop. I would figure ship methods and pricing the next morning.

It was lightly raining as I pulled into the yard the next morning. My man Vince met me at the gate holding several chickens. I noticed they looked wet. He didn't say anything, just walked by me to pick another one off the ground. It was only then that I noticed that there were several lying on the ground all around us.

"What happened?"

Vince shook his head. "Dogs found them."

I walked into my shop and saw chickens lying all over the floor. The large case box was turned on its side. My shop dogs had decided that these chickens were dog toys and they partied like it was 1999 all night long. The chickens laying everywhere had heads and legs torn off and some were just little balls of fuzz. A few of the chickens had the plastic squawk boxes torn out and they were lying about just squawking away for no reason whatsoever. We had to pull the batteries out of those to shut them up.

Vince gathered up the muddy and wet chickens in one pile and the "good" chickens in another. I counted and began to figure I had lost about 60% of my purchase.

"What do you want me to do with them?" Vince asked.

"I will figure that out after a while; just let it rest for now."

I went into the office to do a couple hours of paperwork. I ran out of coffee. When I went into our kitchen I heard the oddest sound I've ever heard. We were a mechanic shop before we were kings of ecommerce, and so some of that equipment was still there. I kept a washer and dryer in the back for cleaning our shop towels and uniforms. That was where my man Vince, who had a stroke of genius, decided to wash the muddy and wet chickens. Only problem was he gave no thought to the electronic squawk box in each one. The noise I heard when entering that area was the sound of about 20 chickens squawking at one quarter speed as they swished back and forth in the washer. Their clucks were slowed down like in a crazy cartoon of zombie chickens.

It was truly horrible to hear.

After my amazement that Vince actually thought this was a good idea, I suggested that he would never get them dry again, and thanked him for going ahead and destroying any value that could possibly be left in them.

On top of this, I later found out that the rubber in the chicken legs was old and beginning to rot. When you pulled the legs out to shoot the chicken across the shop, they just snapped leaving you with a headless, legless chicken.

I finally gave up on this shameful purchase and gave them all to the dogs. They loved them. This is one of the few items I took an absolute loss on. Most items I could figure out how to get some of my money back. Not these chickens though.

Another time, I bought a bunch of fishing rigs. The kind with hooks, floats, swivels, all pre-made. Lots of designs too. I figured I would give them a try. I still have them to this day. I sell about one or two sets a month and have about 2500 sets left. I hope I live long enough to get rid of them all. What made this buy especially bad was that I trusted a vendor who absolutely loaded me up to the eyeballs with inventory. He just shipped it and then hit my credit card. I discovered it when it was already at my shop. It was way over what I would normally have bought. Instead of sending it back, I felt sorry for the guy, plus actually getting a refund would have been next to impossible. I just kept it and tried my best to sell it. Molasses in winter pours faster than these things sell. I was stuck and have been for several years now.

An item we called an ASHNO. Actually it was a pretty good seller. A stand up ashtray with a big red NO on the side of it. We just couldn't figure out how to package it to make it arrive undamaged. I probably warranted half that entire inventory purchase. I even bought stronger boxes and threw the original ones away. No matter, they were just too fragile. Plus if we packed them any stronger the weight increased and then the shipping fee increased to the point we lost money. I wound up donating them to charity.

Pink silicon beehive wigs. My Whoa Factor lit up on these. However, I didn't give much thought as to who my market might be. The result was that they were slow sellers. The sales I did make were always strange too. Like sending several pair to Israel, a few to Alaska, and even to a police department once. The problem that we noticed was the silicon was breaking down and making the wigs stick together.   Maybe it was the heat.   We gave them away finally.

A note on buying close outs.   Many times there is a reason that an item is a "close out."   Meaning that they were simply a bad idea in the first place, or that there is a defect you don't see at first and then later it becomes obvious, or it is the wrong color, or they made too many.   **Problems never show up clearly until you own the inventory.** This is one of the tricks of the trade, trying to figure out if what you have is a simple inventory reduction, a shelf pull, or a total defect that they should have thrown away.   Be on your guard on all close-out purchases.

A further note.   While I'm sure there are some thieves who are selling inventory, you shouldn't blame all these issues on the vendor selling them.   Most I've met are trying to be as straight up as possible.   They realize that if they misrepresent their inventory to you, you may never come back.   All vendors are not created equal though, so when you find one that tells you the truth in advance, stick with them.   Trust is a huge factor in choosing a vendor. They can help you a lot in future dealings.

The list of Shame is long as I have taken many chances in this business. Little did I know that I was actually doing the right thing. Slowly but surely I began to find hits that sold like crazy for a while then tapered off as soon as the market (other sellers) discovered that I was selling them. That is actually a valid strategy.   Study people who sell things kind of like yours, then find suppliers for those things and start selling them. On EBay you start a new listing and price it equal to what the other guy is selling it. On Amazon you just piggyback their listing. Same deal though.   Match their price.   Don't cut price.   It only starts a pricing avalanche to the bottom until you wind up selling your item for break-even or even a loss.

Lots of professional sellers now use automatic repricing software.   You would think this would be a good thing but they still set their prices to be one cent lower than their competitor's price so price fighting continues even to this day.   The only real stability in pricing is when you own ALL the inventory.

8 AVOIDING COMPETITION OR SAILING FOR THE BLUE OCEAN

Imagine the business world as an ocean. Yeah, "Waterworld," whatever floats your boat. The companies fighting for the same piece of business wind up wounding each other then getting blood in the water. Their ocean is always red and represents strife, battle, and stress, price cutting, gouging, pushing and shoving to survive. It is always highly competitive and lends credence to the old saying that business is war.

However, if you look beyond all this froth, you will see a calm blue ocean. You know why? Because none of the killers are over there. The blue ocean is where those without competition live. They don't have to fight every day for every penny because they struck out where nobody else wanted to go. They may not have highly competitive products. Their products tend to be those that don't exist elsewhere because they were created for that reason. The blue ocean represents calmness, serenity, stability, and safety.

I finally figured out that I really hated competition with other sellers. It just always ends badly for the product and my money. I had come to realize the main tenant of my sales philosophy. **Avoid competition**. How to do this? Don't sell what they are selling, especially if there are 20 or 40 sellers selling the same thing? Only a couple of people will make money and even they won't make much. All these people can only hope they have lots of other products to sell to even survive. I'm sure there will be readers wanting to scream out totally opposite opinions. I don't care. This is my deal, how I did it, and still do. Take it or leave it. Or better, mix all the approaches together and come up with what works for you.

So, how to limit or do away with competition? First, I had to own the product. That meant I had to have a contract secure distributorship or that I had to create a product that no one else had or could even get easily, or in the event of a close out, buying ALL inventory available. Then, I needed product that had barriers to entry for competition. For instance it could be large and be difficult to ship, or it could be very heavy and difficult to warehouse and handle. There are lots and lots of other barriers but I use both of these as barriers to entry the most often. Lately, with changing shipping fees based on dimensions more than weight, I am shying away from larger items. Then eventually I wanted product with a name that simply couldn't be copied. So I made a brand name and trademark. Another barrier to those who might want some of my market. I printed branding labels for some of my items to help give them legitimacy. Further, I began to actually print, emboss, and even cast my name into my products. It was a way to separate my items from others.

Speaking of barriers to entry, I know a guy that sells watches. Odd thing is they are name brand and are available everywhere and especially at every big box store. This guy has a unique deal in that he only stocks these brand name watches that are slow sellers. The big box stores don't want to take physical stock of them. Why? They move too slowly. This relatively little guy actually stocks these slow sellers for the big box stores to take orders on. A buyer can always go to a brand name watch company's website, see one of these obscure watches, inexplicably fall in love with the weirdo, and finally ask for one. This guy handles all shipping and handling for these stores. He told me that at certain times of the year he ships 5000 units a day. Seriously cool, as he stocks these for the biggest stores in the world and he's very protected because they don't sell well enough for any of them to actually stock. Genius! He definitely sailed out into the blue ocean.

As for getting a trademark, I did all that myself. I own two trademarks now and the trademark office helped walk me through the entire process. I know that I could have hired expert help for this, but really, it wasn't that difficult. I went to the USPTO.gov website and had to search using the TESS search engine for a trademark that might be used by someone else. You can also search for patents if that is something that interests you.

I was recommended a long time ago to ignore a patent and so far I wish that I had listened to them. I would be $10k richer. I found the patenting process to be tedious, laborious, and very expensive. It may or may not be the right way for you to go eventually but I doubt that I will ever try it again. The lawyer I hired was not upfront about the cost or the procedure so it all kept becoming more and more expensive. I finally bailed. To this day I'm not sure if I had an incompetent lawyer or just a guy who would bill me hours as long as I paid them.

There are many, many experts in all facets of this business. As long as I've been able, I did things myself. Would I have been better off if I had hired outside help? Maybe, but I would have definitely been poorer in money and knowledge. Keeping some of your hard earned money should be foremost in your mind, but not to the point that it strangles your progress. Some things have to be farmed out or otherwise you will waste a tremendous amount of time messing with them. One thing that comes to my mind is graphic art. I have wasted a large amount of time playing with this. I just naturally lean this way so I did enjoy it, but had I just given the job to my buddy Jenny I would have been better off. Everything I spend hours at, she spends 10 minutes.

9 AT A SHOW OR WIELDING THE CASH STRAPPED CHECK BOOK

BUT, how do you get to this point? It all sounds great, except you don't have the products to do these things.

Are you ready to hear what does work and has worked consistently for nearly 20 years now?

Sure you are. It may be the only reason you bought this book.

Prepare

Most modern day buyers use some sort of smart device, be it a cell phone or tablet. Some even bring those lightweight laptops with them. I carried a 10 lb. laptop for a couple years. Thank God tablets came on the scene, if for no other reason than to save my back from carrying them all day. Use your device to look up your finds as you walk the aisles. There are nifty little apps that scan bar codes (UPC) and pull up examples on Google or Amazon. I like to look at both though Google seems to always be higher priced.

Where is your selling market? Mine is mainly Amazon and everybody seems to follow their lead, so I will too. I refer to them constantly when I'm hunting product. At this time I carry my smart phone with excellent camera and an iPad for more detailed search capability. I realize they are basically the same but I can find and read better on the iPad than the phone. Old eyes, I suppose.

I also bring a yellow pad and several pens, plenty of business cards - minimum 50, a copy of my tax exempt or resale certificate (some vendors want proof you are who you say you are), a list of phone numbers in case I need advice on the run, and believe it or not, my elastic back brace folded up as small as it will go and an extra set of glasses. All this crammed into my satchel. I try hard to think of everything. Oh I almost forget Tums, Tylenol and something for bad breath. I also bring several credit cards with as great a purchasing power as I can muster. I even bring a couple of folded business checks. Sometimes they want you to pay on the spot. I have some buddies that won't do that, but if I see something good, I jump on it before a competitor does. Some merchandise is very limited quantity so speed counts.

Dress

I wear tennis shoes, running shoes, or sneakers, whatever they are called now. I will buy a pretty good pair too. Your feet will definitely suffer walking all day. Good shoes will allow you to walk further possibly finding more great merchandise. It's an investment. I also wear shorts in the summer. It's quite hot in Vegas at the fall show. I bring a light jacket for the spring show since it's cooler then. I also bring a baseball cap as my eyes are sensitive to outdoor light. Sometimes you have to walk outside quite a bit from the tram to get to the convention center. The sunlight kills my eyes! I tie it to my brochure bag or satchel. Lots of vendors will give you brochures plus you get the directory they give you when you sign in. You will get paper during the day too. If you don't want to buy a satchel, briefcase, or backpack several vendors will give you free advertising bags when you first get there. Another way to save money.

However, I then promptly spend it at FedEx in the convention center hallway. Instead of carrying around all those catalogs and trying to fly home with them, I just ship them back to my office. I do this at the end of every day. Note that it's about 4 times more expensive than it should be. Not sure why they jack their prices up that way. I suppose the rent is crazy expensive at the convention center so that may be the reason.

Where to Go

I go to the ASD show in Vegas. It is a seriously long lived wholesale buying show that started in 1961. It was named the Associated Surplus Dealers show in those days. Sometime later they changed the name to the Affordable Shopping Destination. I just looked this up on the net. It's so funny that I actually thought the name was the American Specialty Discounters. Sheesh. Guess it doesn't matter that I've had it wrong for years.............

They have over 2800 vendors in several giant halls and 45000 attendees guarantee that these vendors carry everything known to man. You just have to find what interests you. From jewelry, to close outs, to dollar store, to collectibles, to kitchen, to camping, to fashion. The list goes on and on. I admit that I've been to other shows and they are pretty good, but this one works the best for me. There are lots of shows to shop and that information is pretty easy to find on the net so if Vegas is too far check out a closer one.

I know this is Las Vegas! Sin City! Remember that you are there to buy merchandise, not gamble, and go out to expensive places to eat, go to shows, and certainly not to drink and raise hell all night. This will make your buying prowess suffer the next day. Believe me, I know all about it. I'm not trying to be a buzz kill here. I'm trying to save you some money and want you to keep your head on straight. Get up early and be at the doors before they open. Hopefully you have eaten before you come, but if not, take heart in that there will be plenty of food and drink vendors along the edges of the sales areas. All are expensive and pretty much on the scale of airport food but it's part of the price we pay for future success. Still, how many people get to go to Las Vegas to work? You are now one of the lucky few.

Start Walking!

I start at one side of the floor and walk by every single booth. At least I did when I was totally new. I want you to try to do this the first time you go. It will take all day and probably a couple days to complete it. This is part of that education you need to pay for. You will only get ideas doing this and certainly tired feet. The ideas are invaluable. They are where you start to build your business. You will pass booths full of items you couldn't care less about. **Slow down and look at the individual items inside anyway.** Until you look, and I mean look hard, you might miss some great finds. This is your education so slow down and soak it all up. You paid to be here. You will learn to be nice to some sales people and short with others. Don't let them get between you and the merchandise.

Take notes as you go. Sometimes I write these notes on the back of the salesmen's cards. Otherwise I won't remember what I've seen. Mostly I keep a yellow pad with me and make detailed notes there. **If anything looks valuable for future research stop for a moment and write everything that will make you remember the item and the vendor.**

Stop for a moment here. I can't stress the importance of doing this. Maybe describe the booth, or the salespeople, or pricing, or the variety of items. Many of these people will be way more helpful after the show than during the show. Shows can be hectic and very busy so getting a salesman's undivided attention can be difficult. The real problem though is that you will walk by hundreds and maybe even thousands of booths in the next several days and remembering who and what was important is hard. At my age now, it may be impossible!

After all these years, I have developed salespeople who will look out for me as I walk down the aisles. I could share them with you all, but I won't. They are still mine as of this moment. I'm not quite ready to give up the hunt, if ever. Maybe the next book.........

Speaking of the hunt

After all the aisles I have walked I have finally come to the conclusion that I don't want what other people want. I want the last of a kinds. I want the last of a sale item. I may even want a slight defect, or off color, or outright strange item. I once bought a zombie coat hanger plaque, 48" tall, totally weird looking, and I couldn't hardly sell it. People just didn't get it. No matter, it was another education I obviously needed to absorb. It was cool but missed my Whoa Factor. Some things you just got to take a chance on.

Concerning handling defects, deformed, warped, mislabeled........I and my staff have learned to deal with them. We have welded, painted, hung, and bent, adjusted and literally beat on with hammers to repair an item enough to sell. I was determined long ago to fix whatever I got. Even now that we mainly do private label items, we still have to fix some of the inventory that comes in. I've had people suggest that we should just dump this stuff at Good Will or throw it all away. Nah. That doesn't fit my DIY character. I can't forget that I'm the guy that started with a welder and torch making steel fish 20 years ago. If I can fix it, I will.

As I hunted the aisles, I took in dog treats of all kinds and sizes, I took in laser levels in their own cool looking lock box, and I took in sporks made of corn starch that would disintegrate after a certain amount of time. I took in those little cat clocks with their tail acting like a pendulum, of gas masks from WWII, or Masonic pocket knives, or pink play tents for little girls who want to feel like princesses.

I bought a compact floor jack with its own case that fit easily in a car trunk. I bought self-cleaning kitty litter boxes! Some stuff has more Whoa Factor than others. I bought surplus 50 cal. ammunition cans and 1000s of the little springy things that go inside toilet paper holders. I don't know what they are called either.

10 BRINGING THE TREASURE HOME

Coming back to the real world of day to day work can be a letdown after Vegas. I actually do miss the energy and the lights everywhere. I miss the sculptures and paintings, some beautiful and some outlandish. I miss the work ethic of nearly everyone you meet. I miss the entertainment and the fact that a clock doesn't feel necessary.

Still, I can only put my life on hold for so long. When I finally get back I'm ready and excited to get after it, like I'm still carrying some of that Vegas energy with me. I've already mentally researched prices, categories, and search terms, made all my pictures, written my listings and made sure I have the weight and dimensions perfect. My shipping is prefigured and the packaging arranged to make sure the item can make it to its intended buyer safely. Ahhhhh. Let the money roll in...........

However, a few things need to happen first. First, I need to get the pallet (or cases) of stuff from Vegas, or wherever it is in the US to my shop in Houston, Texas.

Many times I can get shipping built into the price of the inventory I'm bringing home. The vendors will use free shipping as a gimmick to get me to commit to a purchase. It works too. Shipping can mess up your cost on an item to the point that it makes it difficult to make a profit.

Keeping your overall cost low as possible is part of the art of this business. For case lots you can use USPS, FedEx or UPS. However, each has its strong and weak points. I've heard many stories over the years about each one and can only relate to you what I have experienced. Understand that different localities may favor one shipper over the other. Then there are myriad other reasons some dislike this one and love that one. This is my view right now from my shop in Houston, Texas.

USPS is great for shipping letters, small packages, flat rate packages, and anything that is relatively close to home. I'm talking within several hundred miles of your location. They are hard to beat. Always double check and compare prices with either UPS or FedEx to confirm that their price on your package is the best. Do this for another reason too. You never stop educating yourself. If you persevere in this business you will become a shipping expert, but you must constantly check and recheck your shipping fees. Don't put this off. If you ship right you make more money too.

Speaking of shipping right, always use the Flat Rate boxes or envelopes with USPS if you can. "If it fits, it ships!" Is their motto. We ship right up to the 70 lb. limit on these boxes and they will deliver them for pretty close to 3 days anywhere in the 48 states. Even more astounding is that they will honor that delivery to Alaska, Guam, Puerto Rico, Hawaii and a lot more for the same money! They are the cheapest and the fastest shipper there is.

UPS is probably the largest package shipper in the US if not the entire world. They are very good and fast and have great people that drive their trucks. However, they do have a negative side. They think they are the pinnacle of shipping and actually were condescending to me a few times. I know that I only ship X amount of packages and yes, I know there are lots bigger companies than us, and yes, I understand that UPS will charge me a weekly or monthly pickup charge, and I do understand that they are doing me a favor to come by at all............ There is another reason I don't do much with UPS and that pertains to their lost and damaged item coverage. They seemed to take forever to give us our credit. It got old waiting. Really, really old.

The last, but most certainly not least, shipping solution for small packages and case lots is FedEx. Again, excellent drivers and support staff from their field reps to their tech people. The main thing that attracted me to them years back was their willingness to pay for their mistakes. ALL companies will have all kinds of problems in the normal course of doing business, but how they deal with them separates the men from the boys. I take care of my customers when any number of weird circumstances occur from an item disappearing in route, to being crushed (with actual tire marks still on the box!) I and my staff won't back down to these losses. Since our reputation is at stake, we normally issue credit immediately. FedEx has stood right up beside me many times in paying for their mistakes or at least figuring out it wasn't their fault.

Another thing that ties me to FedEx is their Customer Appreciation Program. They have supplied me with printers and labels for years, seriously saving me a small fortune. They even gave me a pallet scale once. They do this under contract for a year at a time and I find it well worth it and a wonderful add-on to their normal service.

All those shippers have restrictions so ask them about carrying your stuff. For instance, liquid or batteries may require special packaging or hand holding. Ask first and save yourself some money and aggravation.

If my shipment is bigger than a few cases then I have to get whole pallets (skids) moved. Both UPS and FedEx have LTL (less than full truck load) rates so ask them to quote you. **NEVER just tell them to come pick up your load without getting a quote first!**

I hope I made that clear.

Neither FedEx nor UPS has shown any interest in carrying my pallets. I have asked FedEx several times and was told by a phone rep that they are picky about who they haul for.

Seriously, they told me that.

I'm not sure what I have to do to be taken seriously, other than bend over and take whatever price they want to shove at me. I admit I only do about $4k a month now so maybe that's small potatoes.

An historical note. When I first started hiring trucks to carry my one small pallet at a time, the prices were outrageous. At that old rate I didn't know if I would survive long in this business. I called every trucking company I could get hold of. My memory may be fuzzy now but it seems to me that NONE of them cared if I called at all and would barely give me the time of day. My calls were answered with malaise, sarcasm, and condescension. I admit I knew nothing of the terminology and so could barely communicate with these people. I had no idea of what I was doing. I had no mentors or anyone else to ask about trucking. Google wasn't my friend on this in those days.

About this time I discovered third party shippers. I don't remember how I found them. Maybe they found me as they cold called over the phone. I think Freightquote was one of the first I listened to. They would take my load and direct me to the best deal with trucking companies. If a pallet cost $1300 from a direct query of a trucking company, Freight quote could get it for me for $900. Wow, I was saving a chunk for using these guys! They were always asking me for the class of the material I was moving. I had no idea. Never even heard of it. I asked them what class it should be. They were the experts after all. Everything was fine for a while as I paid approximately $1000 average per pallet. Then, however, my little shipping system hit a speed bump. The trucking company said that I owed them another $1000 on top of the $1000 I just paid due to "re-class."

Somehow, they arbitrarily changed the price of the invoice, AFTER I had already paid it. They insisted I owed them even though I said I didn't. They said I used the wrong class. I pointed out that I had no idea what class the load was and that Freightquote was at fault here. After all, they gave the load a class, not me. It took a while but Freightquote ate that surcharge. I was pleased that they stood up and took care of the problem but they wouldn't quote me for a long time after that. I was forced to look around and man-oh-man I found a jungle full of third party logistics companies. I started sending quotes out to two or three at a time and the price differences were staggering. I would get quotes from $300 to $1500 for the same pallet! Needless to say, I always went with the cheapest one. This tactic has saved me a fortune over the years. Nowadays, I have a list of 6 or 7 logistics companies and I send every quote to all of them. I tell them they are competing and to give me the best price they can. Some stay with me awhile and some quit pretty quick when they never win a quote. **If you don't pay attention to anything else in this book, the previous paragraphs will save you money and lower your cost per item drastically.** Pay attention to it.

Take your cost to ship and divide it by the total pounds you are shipping. It will give you a dollar amount per pound of merchandise. Divide that by 16 and that will give you a cost per ounce. Weigh each item you receive and multiply by the rate per ounce. Add that money to the cost of the item and you will have your true cost with included incoming shipping costs. If you don't do this you will never know your true cost. I do it to this way on every item I receive locally and internationally. **How can you make any money if you don't even know your cost?** You will soon learn that shipping adds a tremendous amount to the cost of your items thereby making your break even higher and harder to attain.

As small time shippers, we are entirely at the mercy of the trucking companies in this country. They typically won't give me the time of day, but will talk to a logistics company. I also let them class my shipments. It's ridiculously hard to figure out. Google "freight class" and see what comes up.

The class system used by trucking companies is horribly complicated and antiquated to the point that whatever they say the class is, even after the load is delivered, is somehow law. Class of an item drastically affects the charges they levy for carrying it. What I'm saying is that they can change the price at any time and demand the shipper pay. One of the strangest ways of doing business ever.

Speaking of law, I looked around and never found a single organization to report these trucking companies. I'm sure there must be someone but I gave up looking. I've even had shipments destroyed by trucking companies. After sending in all kinds of documentation and waiting for a year sometimes, they always say they aren't at fault and I have never received a single refund for damage. There doesn't appear to be any recourse whatsoever. I'm not going to mention any names since every one I've used has had issues. I'm kind of numb to it by now. I have dealt with the remnants of damage several times and managed to sell the items as blemished or scratch-and-dent to get rid of them.

As an aside, about selling scratch and dent inventory, eBay has been really good. I have gotten rid of a lot of inventory time after time on that platform. Knowing the strong points of each platform is quite valuable for limiting your losses. Another thing, **don't think I'm misrepresenting my items to sell them. I don't and I won't.** Believe it or not, there is somebody out there who will buy your scratched up stuff and be totally happy with it. I'm straightforward and upfront about an item's condition. My reputation is at stake and also my good feedback on the platforms. My customers like to look at feedback and deal with reputable companies, just like I do when I'm buying. **Never misrepresent as it will show up in unhappy remarks that stay in your feedback for public view forever.**

Finally one more thing about scratch and dent inventory, be prepared to give it away. I know that sounds harsh, but if it's really bad sometimes you will find that nobody wants it. I give it to charity, Goodwill, as thank you gifts, and even to church. I have found over the years that I can spend way too much time trying to sell an item to the point that I find myself actually reinvesting in it. There has to be a stop point. Discover it for yourself and don't let the bad inventory drive you crazy or fill up your warehouse. That has been a continuing problem for me. I run out of warehouse space! That dead inventory has got to go in some manner.

11 BUYING DEEP

As my business steadied and I found some distributorships along with my pallet buys I really began to concentrate on buying deep instead of shallow. What I mean is that I bought lots of an item after I determined it's the one to buy. I still bought shallow as I applied the Shotgun Approach but I began to be so much more selective. Experience helps with that. The distributorships started with a guy who had invented an aluminum can crusher. I literally called him up and asked if I could buy from him direct. He declined my offer guessing correctly that I was new and small and didn't know what I was doing. I waited a few days and called him again. This time I was more to the point about how many I would actually buy. I offered to buy the huge amount of 4 cases of 6 at a time. This was big for me as I didn't really know if his product would sell or not. He declined again. Finally, desperate to be a distributor for this great item, I called the guy again and offered cash in advance and bumped the initial purchase up to 6 cases.   I was begging at this point.

He finally caved and I went on to buy 20 cases at a time shortly thereafter.   Over time, I asked repeatedly for a better deal to make buying in larger quantities justified.   He never agreed to that and seemed content that I just bought the 20 cases.

I don't know how many years I've sold these particular items; a lot of them.   Unbelievably, he decided to sell direct to Amazon thereby cutting me out.   At that point I decided to quit the relationship and to commit my time and money to items I own totally.   One more reason to private label everything I could.

Shortly after this I got another distributorship with a trash can company.   Competition wasn't too bad as nobody in my market really wanted to sell such a thing and I have since stocked them by the trailer loads for years and years.

I had a couple other distributorships and wound up letting them go since they offered no protection whatsoever to a seller.

I invested a lot of time and energy with these companies by making videos, writing installation and usage script, and handling most of the warranty myself.   I tried my best to be an authority in the field.

As for winning these distributorships in the first place, let me just say I did whatever was necessary to secure them, down to outright begging.   I'm sure any one of these companies when asked would not admit they made me beg, but they did.   I was refused over and over.   Still, I went back to be rejected again. Desperation made me swallow my pride because I knew if I paid the price now I would be repaid for it over and over in the future. I was right too.

If you can lock down a distributorship then by all means do so. It can be the basis of a great living for you. Remember my story about my buddy that sold watches? Just make sure you get a contract if you can. At least make sure they will limit how many distributorships they will make. Try your best to get an exclusive. If you do get it, give it everything you have to keep the company happy. The payback can be tremendous.

Buying deep allowed me to get my shipping costs way down. It allowed me to compete with just about any competitor. I began to get free shipping deals when I was in Vegas because I bought so much. Things were getting sweeter.

However, just as I would get an item moving in the market it never failed a competitor would show up (sometimes the vendor I actually bought from in the first place) and the price would begin to fall. In the beginning they would cut my price, then I would cut their price in retaliation. They followed with another cut, and so did I. We generally did this till we found the bottom dollar we could sell at. Sometimes I would just take my merchandise out of the market and wait. Sooner or later they might run out of merchandise. This works fine if you are dealing with limited items, but if the item was made to sell this way, they would simply make some more and continue to compete. Hopefully my original investigation uncovered that before I bought it. In spite of due diligence I would get caught this way sometimes. I grew to hate it too. Generally, unless there was a great explanation, I would never buy from a vendor that did business this way again.

A salesman contacted me and I agreed to buy some animal traps to see if I could sell them. They were the lightweight wire live trap kind that didn't hurt the animal. I did my research and didn't see many online in any market that could compete with the price he was offering me. I bought a bunch of them. While I couldn't buy all of them (they would simply order more) I could buy them under $10 and sell them in the mid $30s. I would give them a shot. I sold a lot of them on both eBay and Amazon. I was buying them pallet after pallet. One day I notice that the normal number of sales hadn't materialized. Something was wrong. I searched online and found a competitor.

This competitor was not only beating my price, he was selling the traps for damn near what I paid for them. I did some investigation and found out the company I was buying from had set up a selling account for their children and this was one of the items they decided to let them sell. I was astounded and angry and told the salesman all about it. He was totally embarrassed and helpless to do a thing other than complain for me. They basically gave me the finger and I had to cut price to cost to get rid of the dead merchandise. I marked it down and gave some to charity. At least something good would finally come from this item. As for the company that had it manufactured, I vowed to cease this type of business on my end from this point forward and never deal with them or anyone like them again. Those companies are simply too stupid to deserve my business.

12 BUILDING A BRAND (IT'S FUNNY HOW THINGS WORK OUT)

My company was originally DC Mach Tire.   It was derived from a band I was in long ago.   "DC Machine." Very 80's sounding, eh?   I changed it again to DC Mach Inc. when I incorporated.   I was trying my best to be legal and sound important and bigger than I actually was.   I've been in business since 1987 and have never had more than 5 employees so size never really happened. Now, I'm changing the name again to Carvers Olde Iron (our main brand) to more reflect what we sell and to give our company a little more interest at first glance by a buyer.

Way back when I first hired employees the whole vibe of my business changed. While I was always trying to expand and take on new jobs and opportunities, I began to stress about keeping my guys busy and keeping my shop afloat. With the effect of desperation, I began to consider all kinds of work totally outside my realm. I had also begun to tinker with my torch and welder. I have always been artsy fartsy anyway. Ok then, more on the fartsy side, believe me I've heard it all. The effect of my looking outside my current circumstance to better pastures was about to prove itself again.

One day a customer came into my foyer and looked at some of my fabrications and said he wished I could make steel rings for him. That light bulb thing you see in cartoons appeared above my head. I told him that I thought I could make them. How many did he want? He told me that he used them constantly and that it would be a continuous need. My interest went up another click. I told him to give me some time and I would get back to him. He was grateful I wanted to do this. I was on it! I needed this work. I had bought a tire splitter machine some time back from a repair shop that had closed down. We tried splitting tires with it but it just didn't work that well. However, it was super strong and so had plenty of raw power. I took it apart and fabricated some rollers and bearings, a couple stops, a foot pedal and poof; had a ring maker. Going back and reading this makes it sound like it was nothing, but seriously it was a brain twisting experience because I didn't have any money to throw away if this thing didn't work. Plus, I had never done anything like this. I can't express how delighted I was to form my first ring out of 3/8" steel rod. Even my guys were delighted as it certainly looked like it would brighten my sour face a bit.

Thinking back I had built a remarkable little machine once before though having no experience whatsoever. I was in junior college. Someone remarked that I appeared to be pretty handy but I had no business messing with a loom.

There was a loom in the room that they purposely kept away from us lesser human beings. I was a part time model for the art classes. Who knew that string-thin skinny guys would be in demand in the art world? Actually all the body types were in demand and I simply filled in one of the slots. This job allowed me to hang with the art students and all the cool stuff they did. What they didn't know was that I had full access to a wood shop in the theatre, which was my major. I promptly went down and spent a couple days and built a working loom. Did it work perfectly? Probably not, but it worked well enough that the instructor kept it to show off. I don't know what happened to it after that. I did weave a couple hand bags with it first though. Even back then, just because I didn't know how to do a thing didn't mean I couldn't do it. I just hadn't gotten to it yet.

I called my customer up and he said bring some of the rings over. Hmmm, I noted a lackadaisical reply to my enthusiasm. I carried a bunch of rings over and walked into the dirtiest, nastiest, piled up filth of a shop I have ever been in. My first thought then was, I don't think I'll give these guys any credit! They invited me into the office which was no cleaner than any other part of the place. I was careful not to rub up against anything and that's saying something since I came directly from a working mechanic shop. They took the rings, thanked me, and said they would get back to me.

I heard nothing for a week. Finally, I couldn't stand it any longer. I risked another visit to their disgusting shop. I walked in on them forming their own steel rings with the most dangerous system anyone could imagine. They bolted a frame on their forklift wheel, then inserted a steel rod, then jacked up that side of the forklift and put the transmission in drive.......very slowly. Hopefully the ring they were making didn't jump off and try to kill somebody as it sprang across the shop.

They gave me all my rings back except one that they used as a model to make their bender. He told me thanks for the sample.

I was speechless and embarrassed. I had just spent a ridiculous amount of time building this ring making contraption and now this D--khead blithely declined it. I fumed and I moped for a few weeks. Finally, I went to my pile of test rings and began to stretch them out, trying to figure a use of some sort. Maybe I could salvage something out of them. Dejected and as usual desperate for a win, I bent one a certain way and magically saw the shape of a fish materialize. I grabbed a hammer and then finally a torch and poof, to my eye, it was a fish. I was surprised to say the least. I never knew I could make any kind of sculpture.

Stranger, and still something I've never explored enough to really understand, the shape of a fish has always kind of been my spirit animal (if there is such a thing!). A fish has always represented the good part of this world to me. Where there are fish, I've felt safest. It was only appropriate then that it was a fish I saw in that first sculpture.

Back to my ring failure. I began to utilize those rings in all kinds of fabricating ways. I made not only fish, but weathervanes, signs, wall sculptures and even free standing sculptures. I was totally surprised that I could sculpt anything at all. I discovered I actually had an eye for it. Who knew? This was another great learning lesson in my life. **Just because I don't know how to do a thing right now, doesn't mean I won't be good at it in the future**. Again, I just haven't gotten to it yet. So, it wasn't a failure at all.

During the middle of this steel ring enlightenment, I built the A30 Hickey Bar. This is a hand tool I built with the insistence and support of my longtime friend Doyle Odom who was also my next door business neighbor.

I bought the property I started on next to a guy I barely knew, but liked. One of the prime reasons too was that his first name was Doyle, a relatively rare first name. We decided on the spot we should be neighbors for that, above all other reasons. Later on, he was also in my wedding as a groomsman.

He showed me how to shape the head and the placement of the studs that go in it. He said he would buy them from me if I made them. This particular model didn't really exist on the market as most swimming pool installers just built their own.

I didn't know it but this was the start of my career as creator and not a distributor of another person's stuff. It would be my first rule of business in the future. Second rule, find an item that is undersupplied or doesn't exist. Third rule, change it, make it unique. Fourth Rule, make it better. Note that all these rules are quite flexible and interchangeable and all required for my business private label.

When I first started building these hickey bars they were all totally handmade and tedious and slow. Sales were slow too as the Internet wasn't really everywhere yet. Many of my customers didn't use the net at all. They found me by word of mouth.

After all these years I will still have an old Hispanic man, burned dark brown by his time in the sun, stop in and buy a couple hickey bars. Not a word of English has ever been spoken between us. I've never understood it exactly. Men like this are scared of no kind of work in any element and go with pride to do it seven days a week if need be. They will do anything for their families who make all this labor worth it. But they can't speak English even after living here 20 years. It has to be a terrible disability, yet they struggle on. These men are easy to admire even if they do make me shake my head in wonder.

I've sold those hickey bars for so many years I don't remember when exactly I started making them. With time though and listening to customer inquiries, I have added different models to that line. Plus when the Internet caught up with my little manufacturing company it helped me make larger production runs thereby cutting my cost. I even had a custom sticker made that goes on every bar. I now make five different styles and sizes of hand benders, a rebar jack, and a bench bender. At one time I even built the headache racks for the trucks but gave that part up. Everything we do now can be shipped via FedEx or USPS.

After this rather slow take off I began to make all kinds of steel sculptures. I couldn't seem to get many that would bear much production though. I mainly built steel fish, horseshoe sculptures, and a few signs. One interesting job I managed to get through Internet notoriety was a frame of a Santa Claus in scuba gear. Plus it was about 10' tall.

Then I had to make it to disassemble so it could ship on a pallet. It was part of a lighting display in a water float in New Mexico. It was fun. One more use of my new found drawing/sculpting talent.

Perhaps the only art item I've kept from all the fabricating has been making our 23" Giant lure spoon. We sell it year round even to this day and still fabricate, paint, and assemble in house.

During this industrious effort was when I started distributing aluminum can crushers. I have always loved gadgets and what better gadget than one that crushes aluminum cans for economical storage and pays you back at the same time? I sold these for years and was a self-described recycling expert for quite a while. As with most things I didn't own, the manufactures sold out or changed policies or sold direct to Amazon making their items have tremendously less value for me. Sadly, I had to sell out and do away with them. I actually became emotionally invested in some of these items, so it really is difficult to leave them. Sadly enough, in the end, I didn't leave them as much as they left me.

However, during this withdrawal I saw a need for another better, more unique can crusher that would serve a part of the market that was ignored. My old manufacturers didn't do away with me, they wound up making me!

The MasterCrush Aluminum Can Crusher was born. We designed it to fit the largest cans on the market and be smooth to operate and be repairable in the field if need be. This unit is designed to last for years and years, not just the season. As for being repairable. Let's face it, everything -and I mean everything will break. I designed my can crusher with replaceable parts. It will last nearly forever, though I only give it a 90 day warranty. If it's going to break due to defects or workmanship, then it will happen in 90 days. Over that, then it will generally be abuse. It's amazing what I have had buyers tell me they have tried to crush with it. Warranty won't cover cat food cans, bean cans, coffee cans, or any steel can. These buyers know when they've messed the unit up and gladly buy another one.

About this time I designed a flag box that opens from the front and a wooden novelty fishing reel that holds a roll of toilet paper. Both items sold ok, but no gang busters.

I mentioned that I built little sculptures out of used horseshoes. I had a call list of farriers from all over this immediate area. I tried my best to keep them in stock too, but the farriers kept running out of used shoes. At one time I was buying them by the trailer load wherever I could find them. I had slowly built a small market that needed these shoes and just ran out of stock. What a shame to build a market from basically nothing and then run out of stock over and over again. I even doubled my purchase money but the farriers didn't seem to care. Finally, trying anything to keep my little market working, I sent some used shoes to a vendor overseas. He made me buy the molds and then produced a test run of a few hundred of each size. Thank goodness it worked and my little sculpture crafting market stayed intact.

I also found some close-out buckets at one of the trade shows. I discovered that I could sell a few. Same thing happened as the horseshoes. I kept running out of buckets. So, I started making buckets for gardening and crafting and then added standing ashtrays, then bookends, doorstops and finally complete bathroom accessory sets. I'm sure I'm leaving stuff out as I consider finding, making, designing product my main job now. I'm pretty sure the future holds nothing but Carvers Olde Iron merchandise. It's more than just ego at work here. Having my own private label is tremendously more stable as a business. While I do have trouble with production I don't have to worry about someone else cutting my prices or running out of stock or loading me up with more competition. I seek the blue ocean.

I shy away from competition as a general rule of thumb, but sometimes you just can't help it. When that happens, say, I make a particular bucket only to find the market has 6 more of them that look just like it. I then start trying to make mine unique. Maybe have my name emblazoned on the side, or add creases to it, or make a different handle with wooden holder in it. I will change my bucket around till it has no competition. At that point I don't care what the other guys are doing.

Note that I do this on just about every item I have. I have no direct competition that I can think of. Of course I do have competition with all the other buckets in the universe, but at that point it depends on the utility, or the looks, or something else. I just want a spot on the world merchandising stage. My item sells or it doesn't. If it doesn't, I go to the next item. As I follow the strategy of the Blue Ocean and make stand alone items I will just naturally avoid the blood lust of price cutting. I do have to pay attention to what all the other buckets sell for but I don't have to fight them for pennies.   There is plenty of businesses out there that do live for that type of ecommerce combat, but I'm not going that way and you don't have to go that way either, unless you just love the battle.   If so, go for it.

I mentioned earlier that I certainly don't have all the answers to this business.   I just have a small, almost infinitesimal, slice of the pie.   As a small business this is enough for now. My goal was attainable and I reached it. Feels pretty good too. I hope no one minds that I revel in it for a while.

13 THE SOCIAL SIDE OF THINGS.

While my products can always be found in a search, if you are determined enough, I wanted to have buyers interested in them as a way of life. Yeah, horseshoes rule! - or ashtrays, or aluminum can crushers, or buckets, etc. Still, as dumb as that sounds, the people who buy such things are a hands on group and need a place to gather. In my mind, my website should be the perfect spot. As I got more and more established I realized that other venues own control of just about all my customers. I found that getting them to move over to my site is difficult and time consuming. Does that mean I won't continue that direction? No. I'm still going there, albeit slowly. I'm adding to my online social standing every chance I get. I suppose I could have included this in my branding chapter, but really this is a standalone problem.

So, I made a Facebook page for my company and tried to update it every so often. I had a miserable start and stop procedure that I don't recommend.   I had very little to show for my efforts after a year or so.

During this time I also blogged or my version of blogging anyway.   I wrote little short stories and added links to sympathetic sites.   Yep, it was a miserable flop also. I did wind up with some cool writing out of it.   Otherwise I don't think it added one thing to my overall goal of being found online.

I also made some YouTube videos and have gotten quite a few views.   I included a link back to my site.

Still, I am the guy that makes product and that is my forte.   I find that the more I stray from that part of my job, trying to teach myself something new, the more I regret it. Recently I found a company to help me.   98buck social. They literally go online and post for me on Facebook and Twitter.   They do this every few days and so far I'm happy with them.   One very smart thing they do is post things that aren't exactly about me or my product.   After a while, once my buyers have my products stuck in their faces repeatedly, they will develop a kind of blindness to them.   It happens to me when some company sends me too many marketing emails.   I just tune them out.   So this company helps by talking about the DIY community, crafters, collectors, design, and even philosophy.   All this is very easy to absorb when a visitor comes across it.   I will stay with them this next year.   After all, there are only so many sales pitches anybody can stand.   It is human nature to shut them out or just flat run away from them when they become repetitious.

One side benefit of this social help company is that it keeps my Facebook page foremost in my mind.   Now, I will add to it occasionally and also more things to my website.

For instance, I now have a section devoted to publishing short stories of my customers. I include their pictures and showcase what they make.

My business has a lot to do with hands on type people. The art and craft they make is what I call folk art. Their designs and end products are learned from each other and passed around freely.

Anything I can do to help them do that, I will. I'm planning some hands on videos soon to show some techniques we use in working with this stuff.

14 MY FUTURE

Some time back my business grew to the point that it just wasn't me doing it all anymore. I hired a helper who took some of the welding, painting, packaging and even brainstorming off my plate. Then later as I could afford it, I hired a lady to help in the office. She was my right hand girl for quite some time until to my crushing disappointment, she embezzled my company. Yeah, it took a minute to get over that. My most trusted employee ripping me off? I felt my judgment sucked and became more determined than ever to pay more attention to the details that I actually don't care for. I've always hated telling people what to do.

Finally, I've survived long enough to be able to bring my wife and partner into it. She now handles all the day to day office and shipping. I always wondered if I could ever make enough money to hire her and consider it a great testament and blessing of how well we are doing. She is a serious workhorse and loves this work as much as I do. Our measure of success is different from a lot of other companies, I'm sure. Working together was one of them.

One thing that has changed in our relationship is that we sit together and say a prayer at home before work every day. We are a bit amazed at ourselves but find that it starts the mental part of the day so much clearer. We always give thanks for our blessings and we do it every single day.

The company will continue to grow mainly through added private label product. It is the most fun thing in the world to develop product. The Internet has allowed me to avoid some social interaction, which I'm thankful for, but also given me equal footing with some very large sellers that, otherwise, I would never have had a chance to compete.

I remember, that it wasn't very long ago, I was painting USED TIRES on the side of a big truck tire tube and hoping somebody, anybody, would see it when I placed it by the street. I remember those small baby steps well. They were the price I paid, my tuition, my working man's schooling. I hope that I have told you enough to get you started if that's what you want. You will have to want it bad to make it all worth it. Of course, I can't tell you everything that's going to happen but I warned you as best I can through my desperate stories. Take what you can here, add your stories to it, and remember to give it to someone else down the line.

Never forget, we all needed a hand up somewhere-- way back.

May God bless you and yours.

DCC

January 21, 2018

Visit: **www.carversoldeiron.com**

Or email: **doylesee@sbcglobal.net**

The simple truth about how ordinary people accomplish outrageous feats of success is that they do the hard things that smarter, wealthier, more qualified people don't have the courage ----or **desperation**---to do…

Dan Waldschmidt

89650840R00065

Made in the USA
Columbia, SC
23 February 2018